This book belongs to

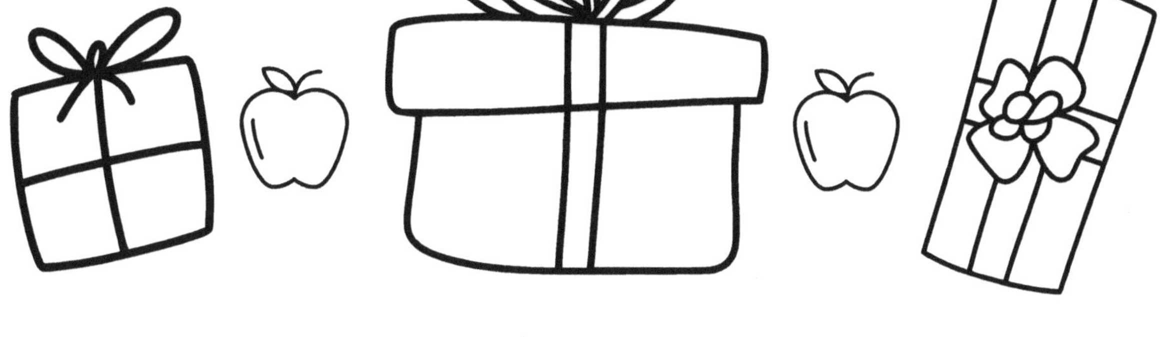

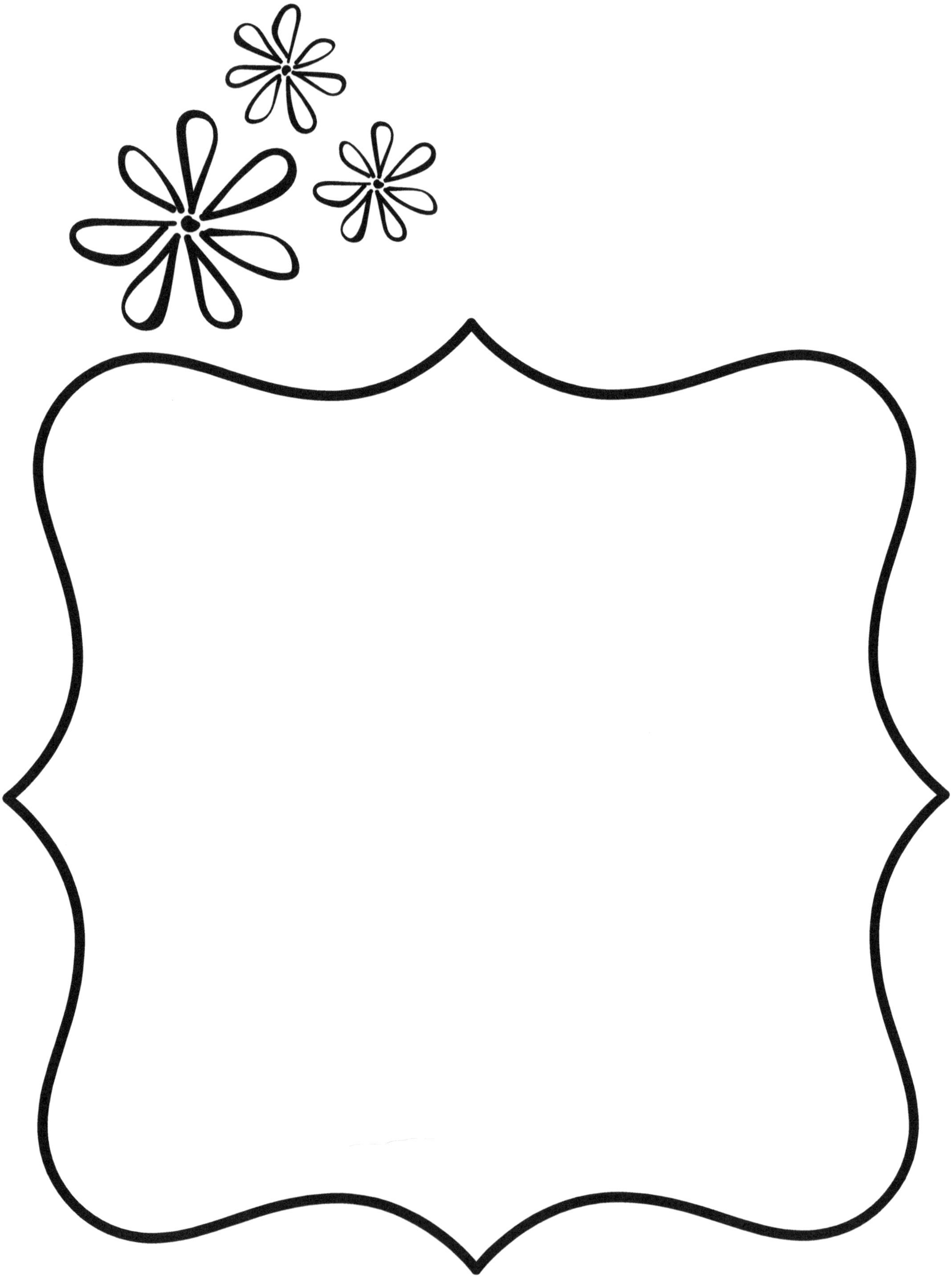

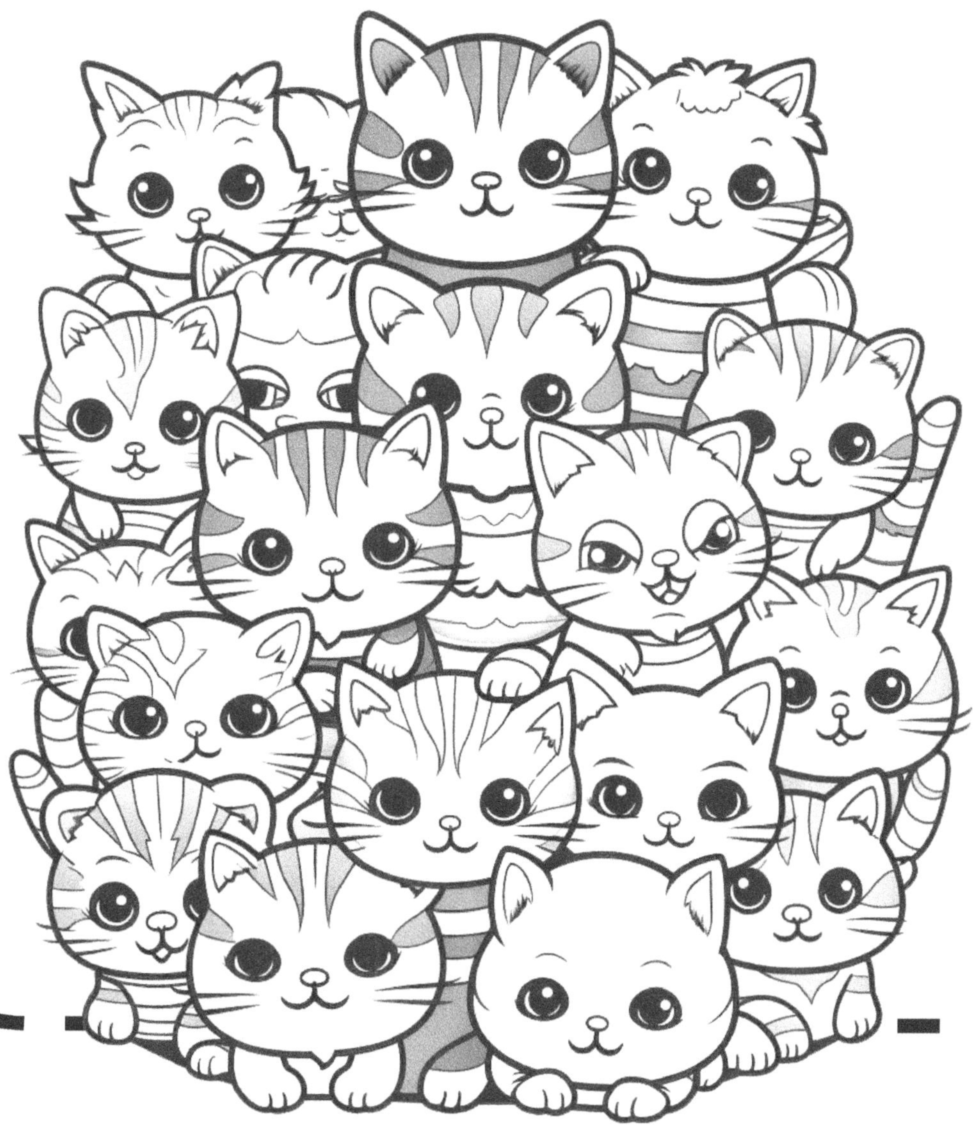

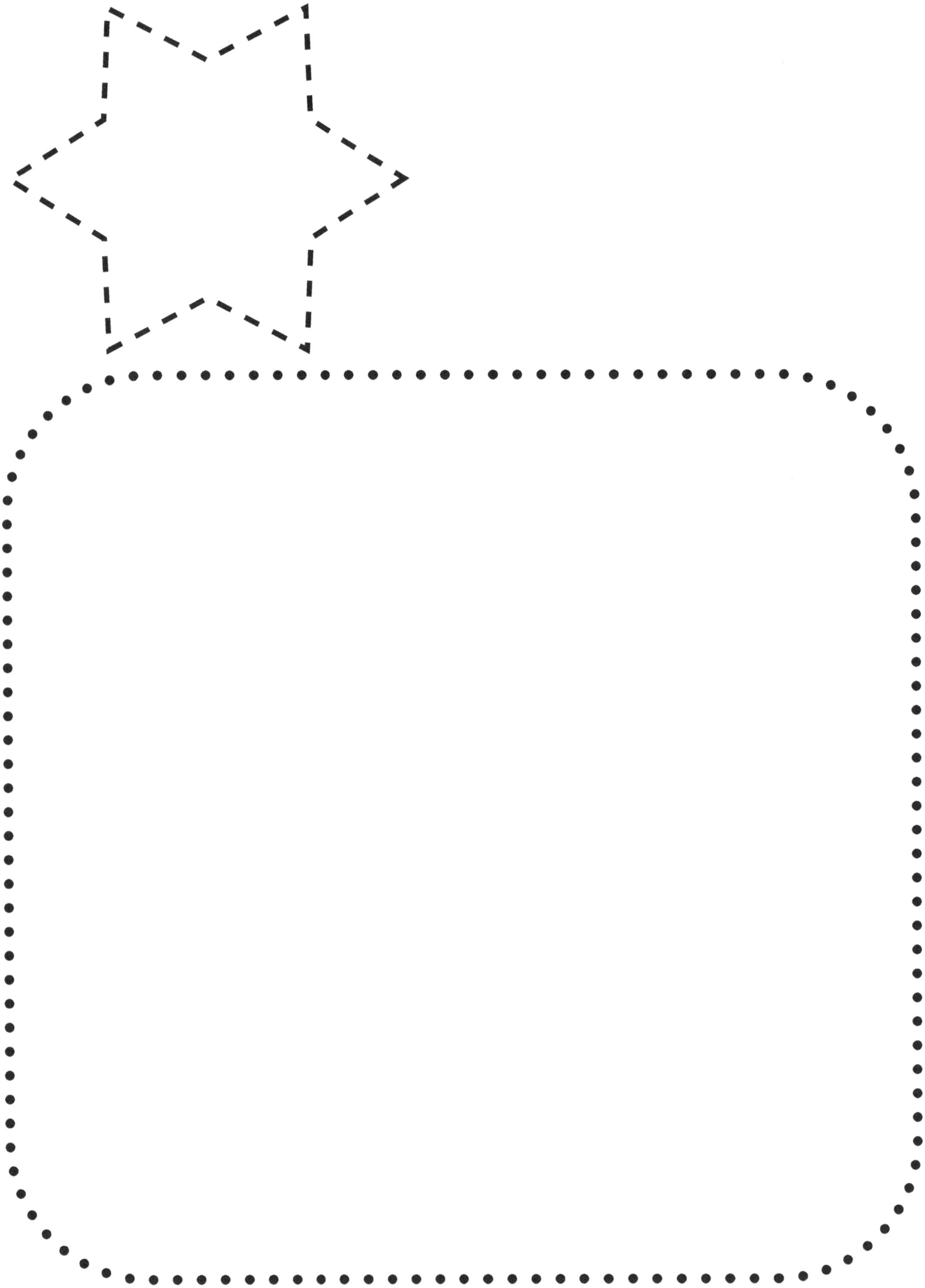

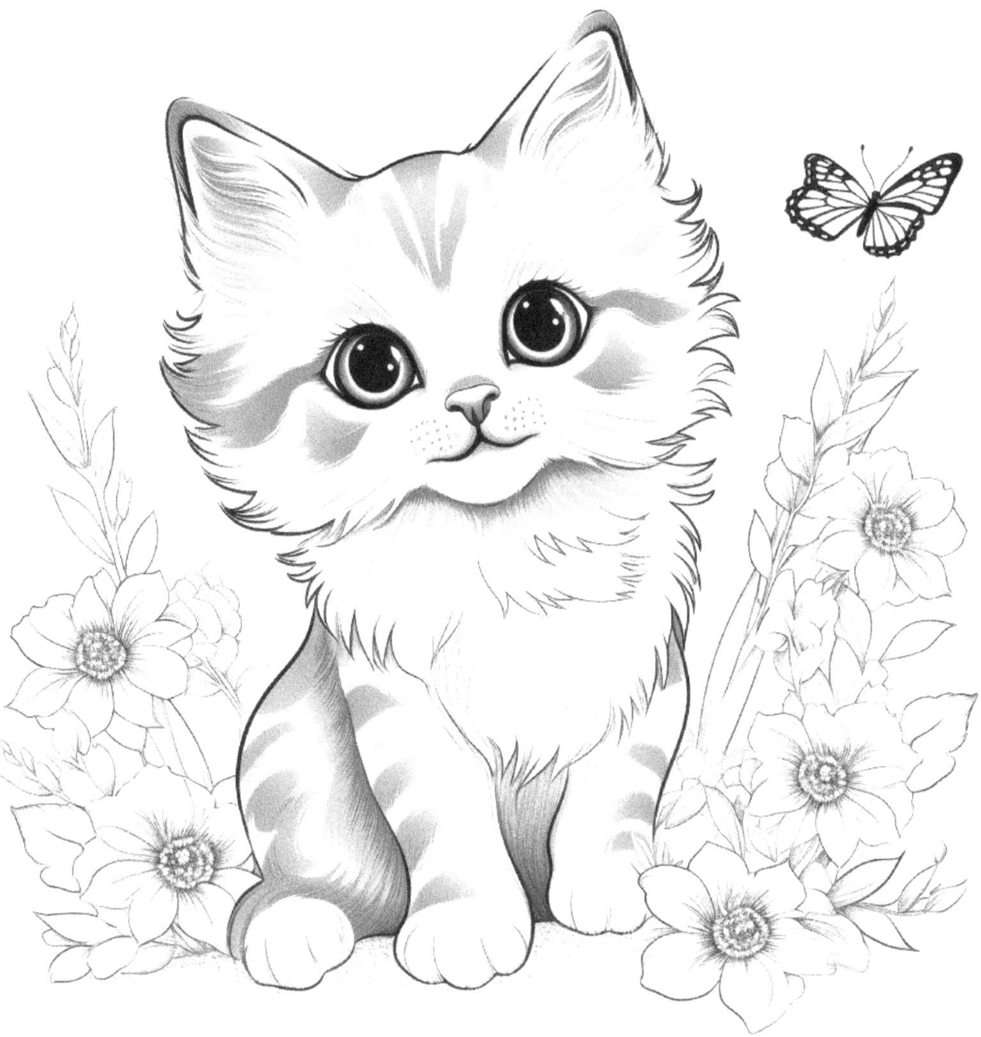

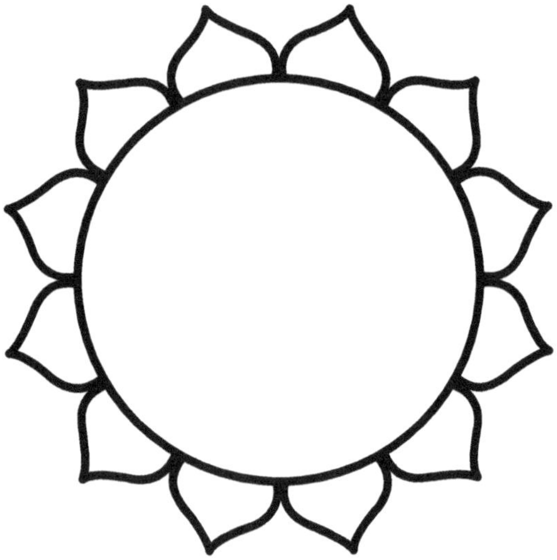

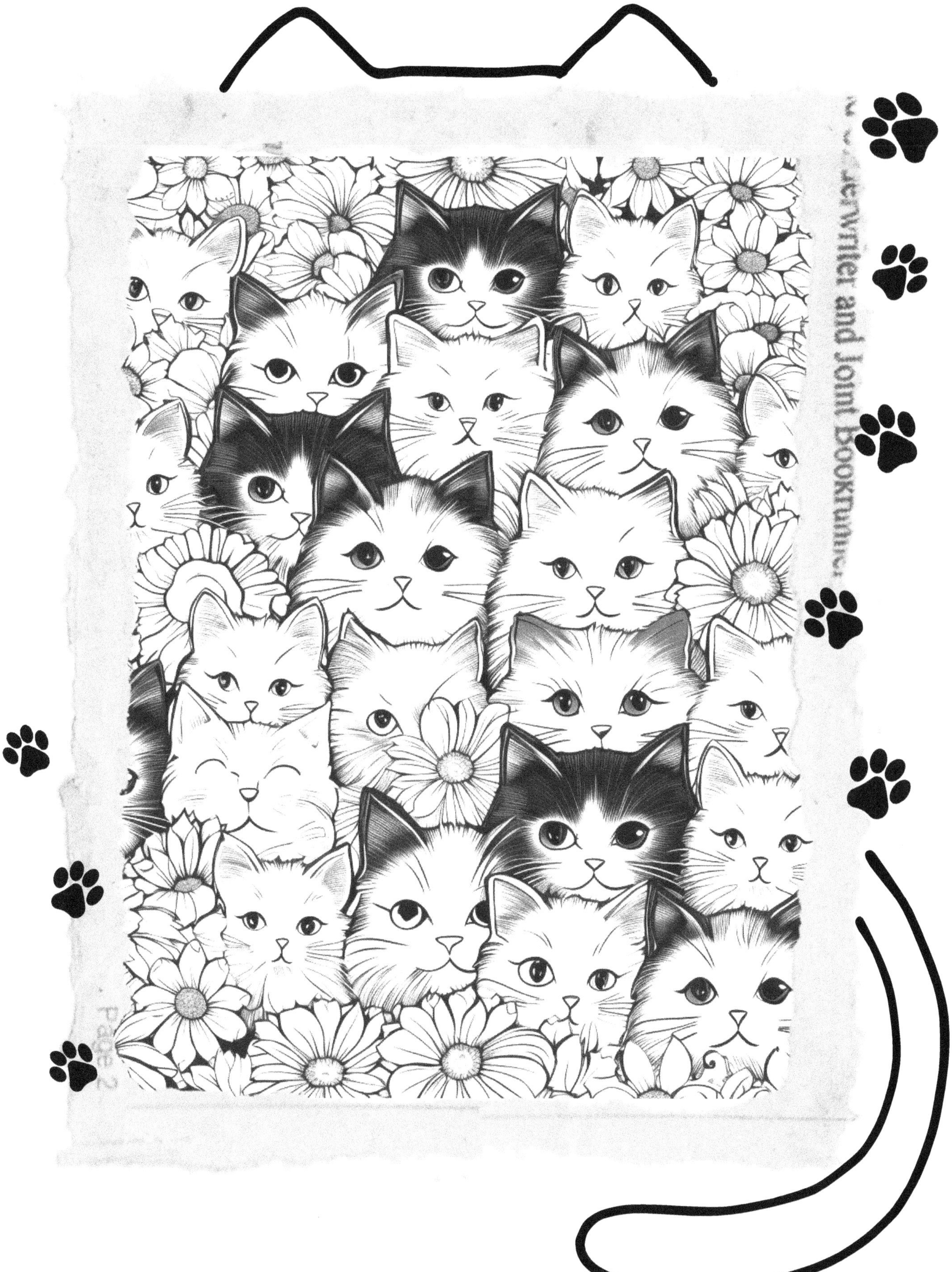

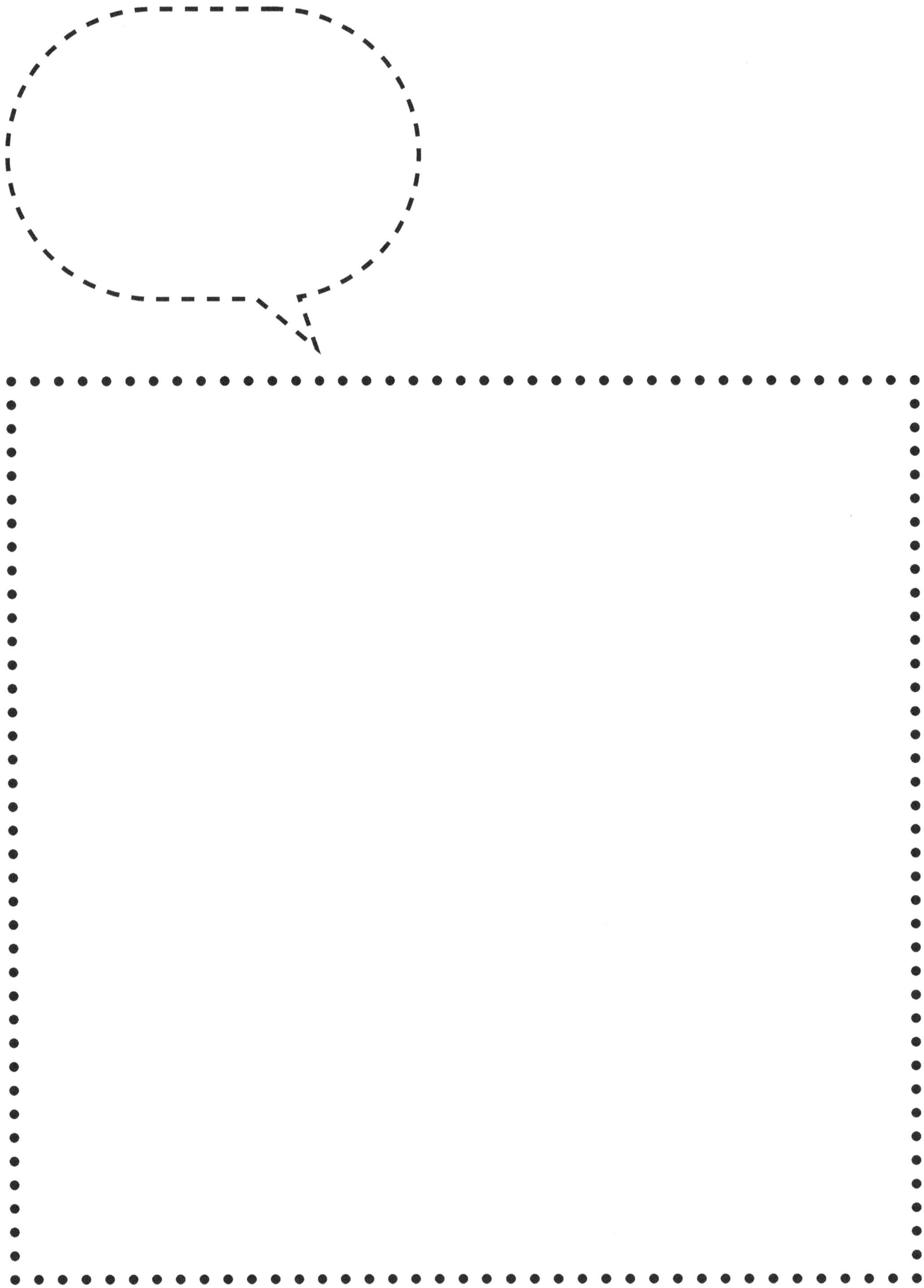

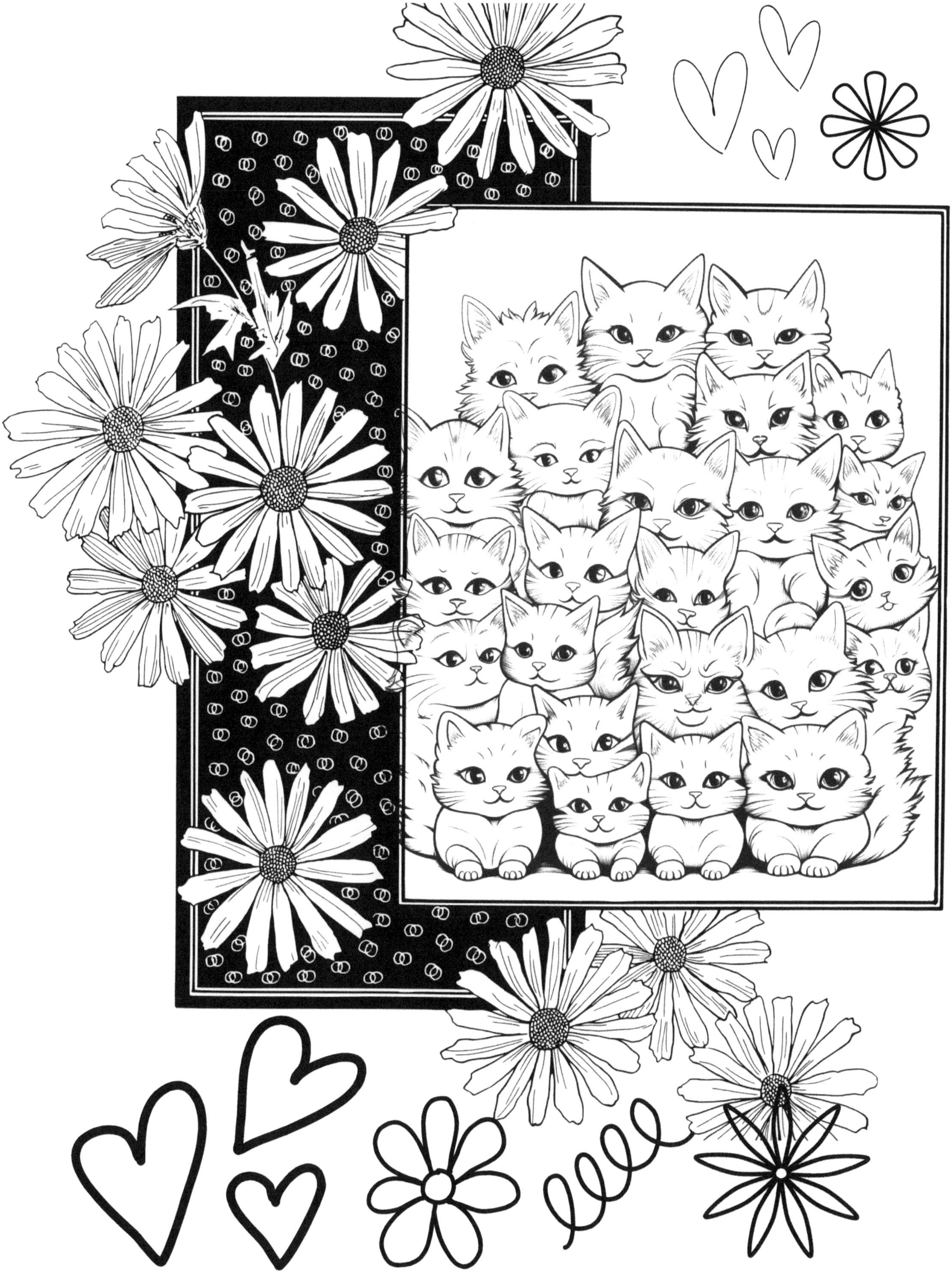

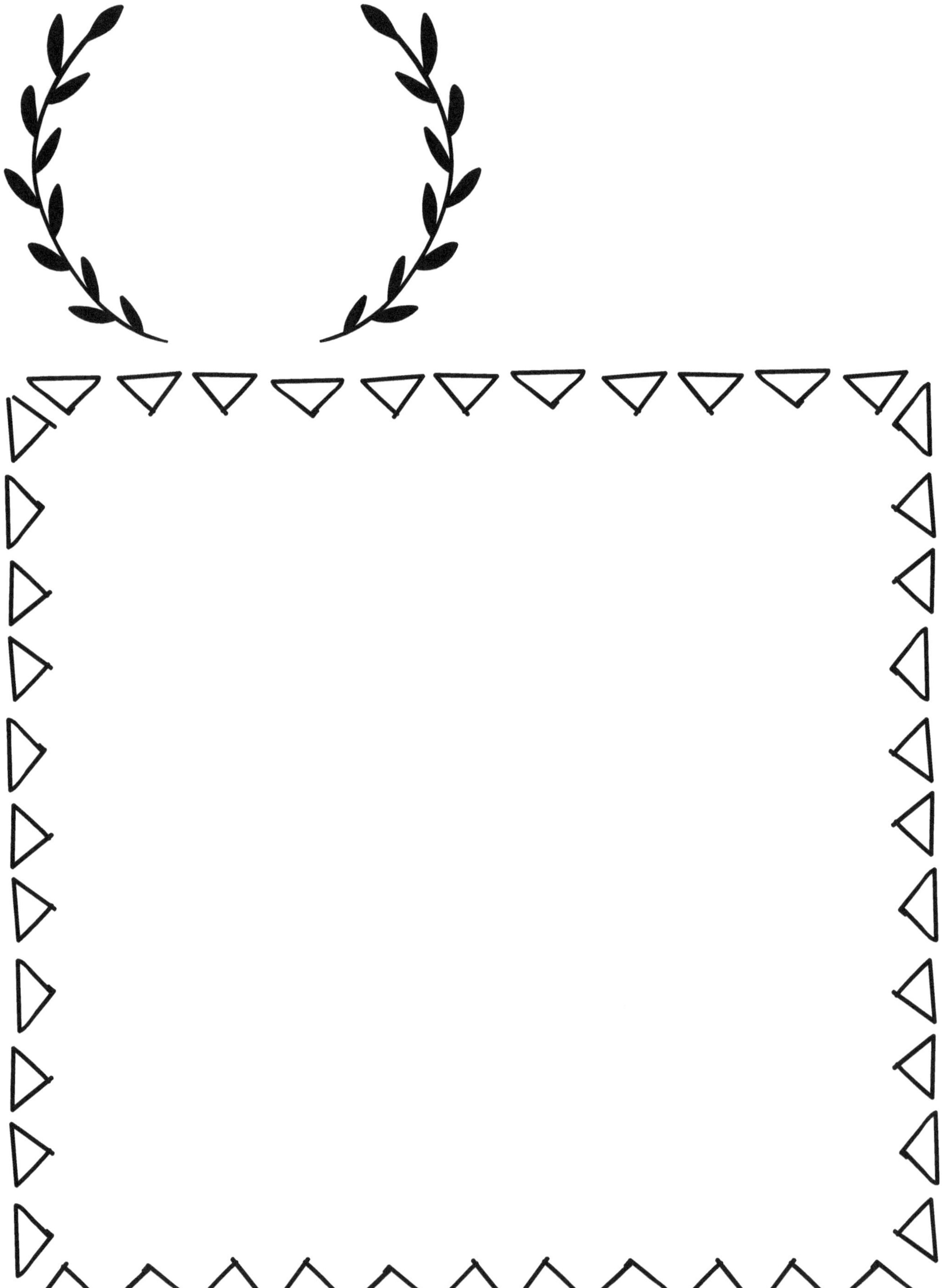

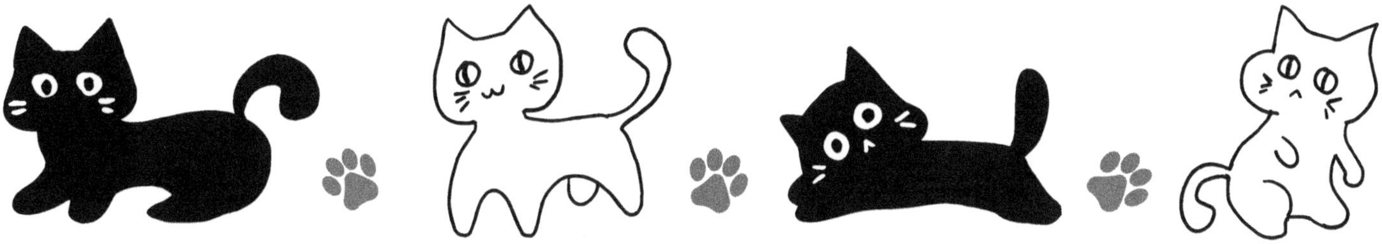

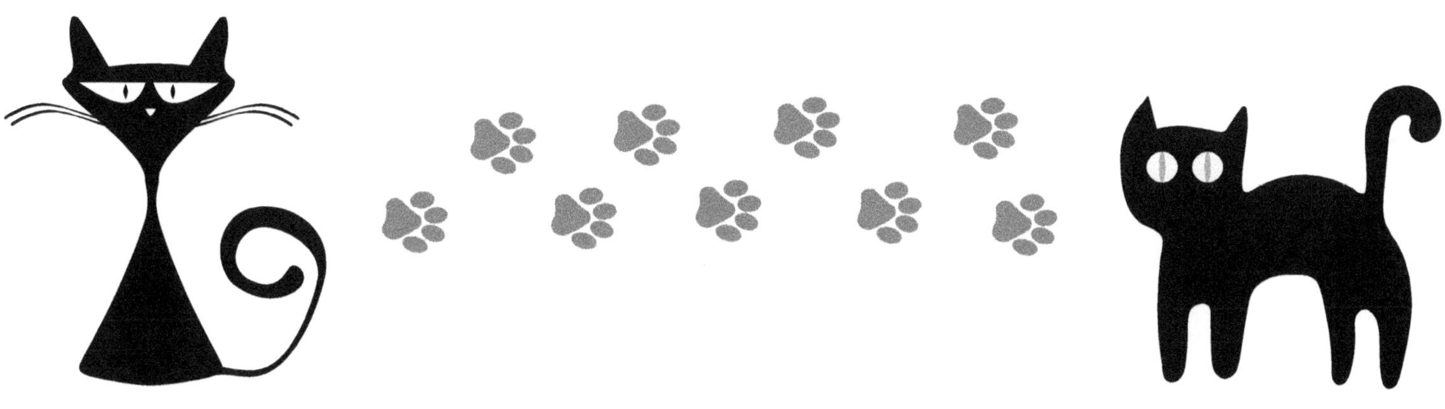

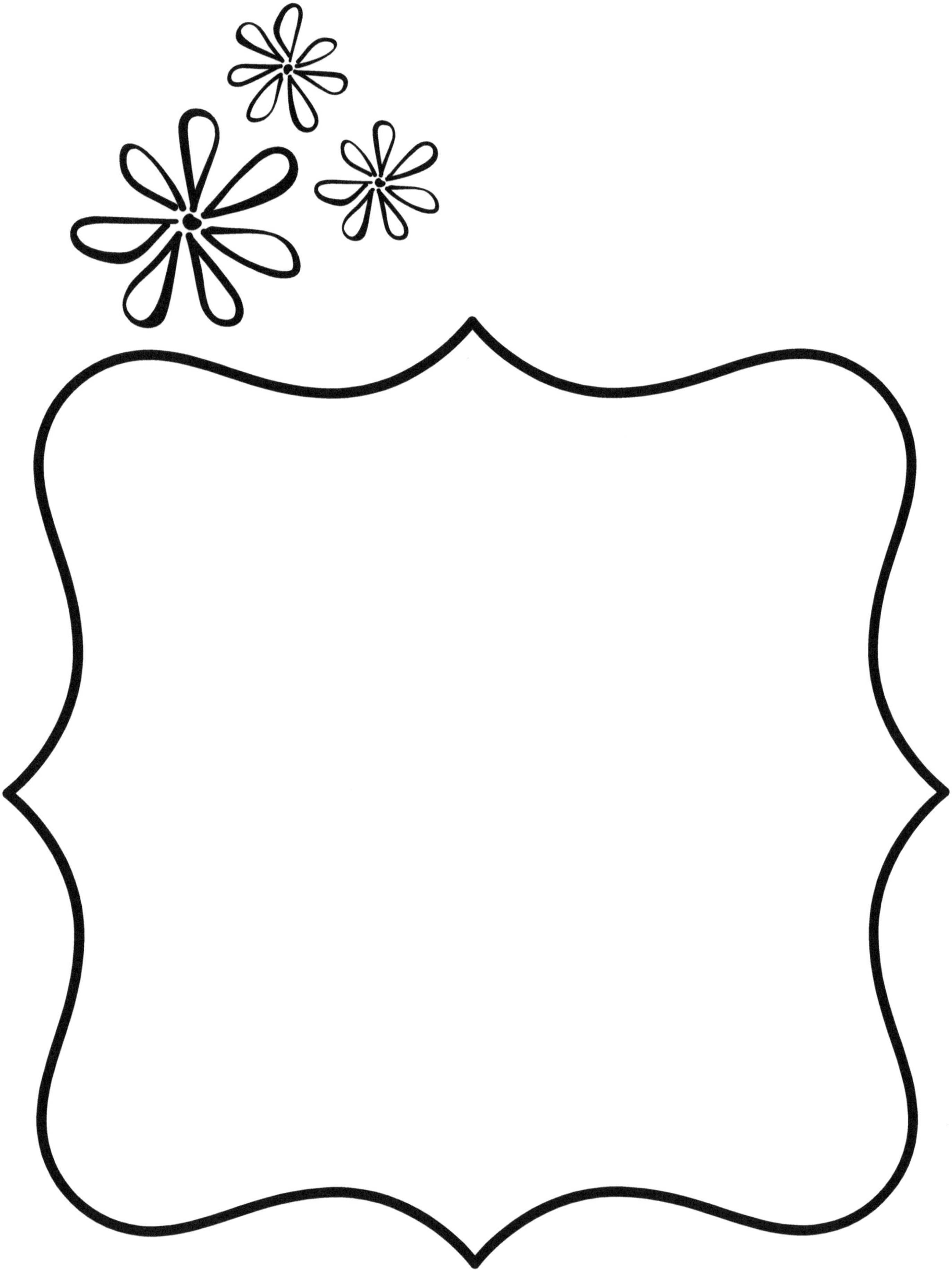

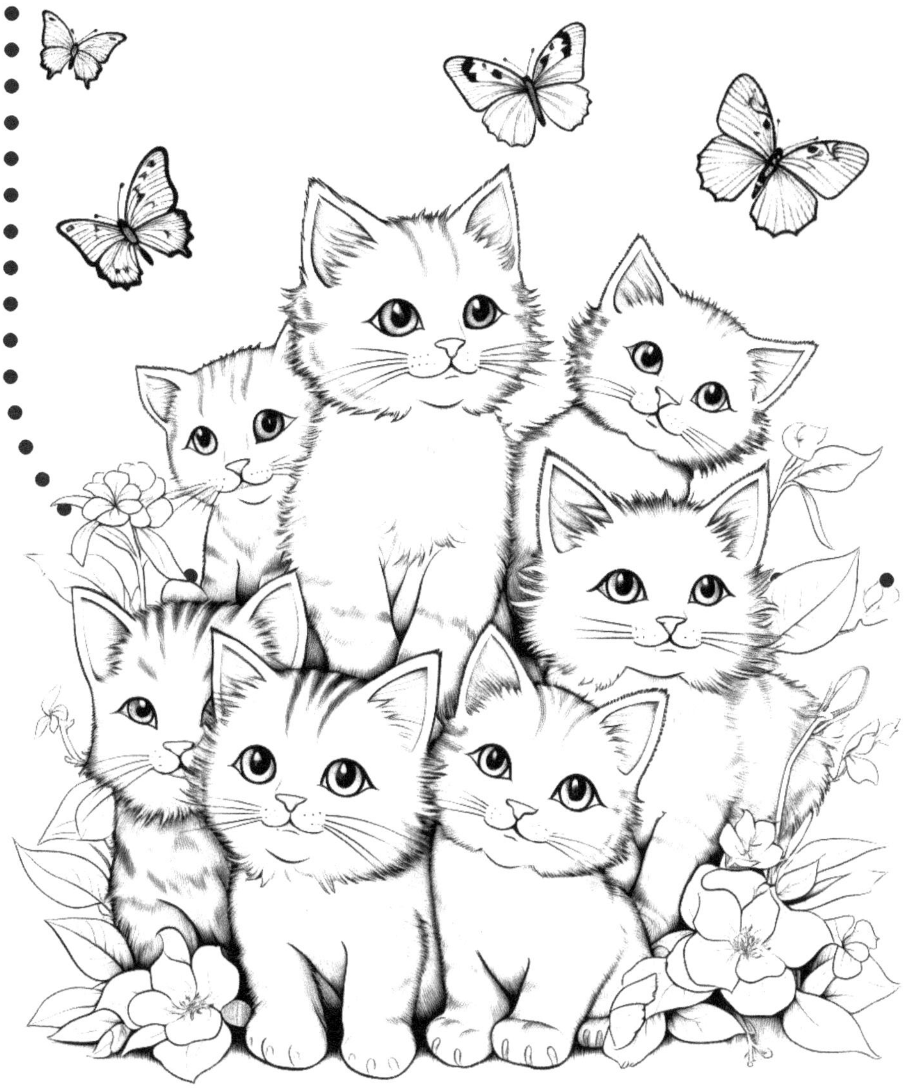

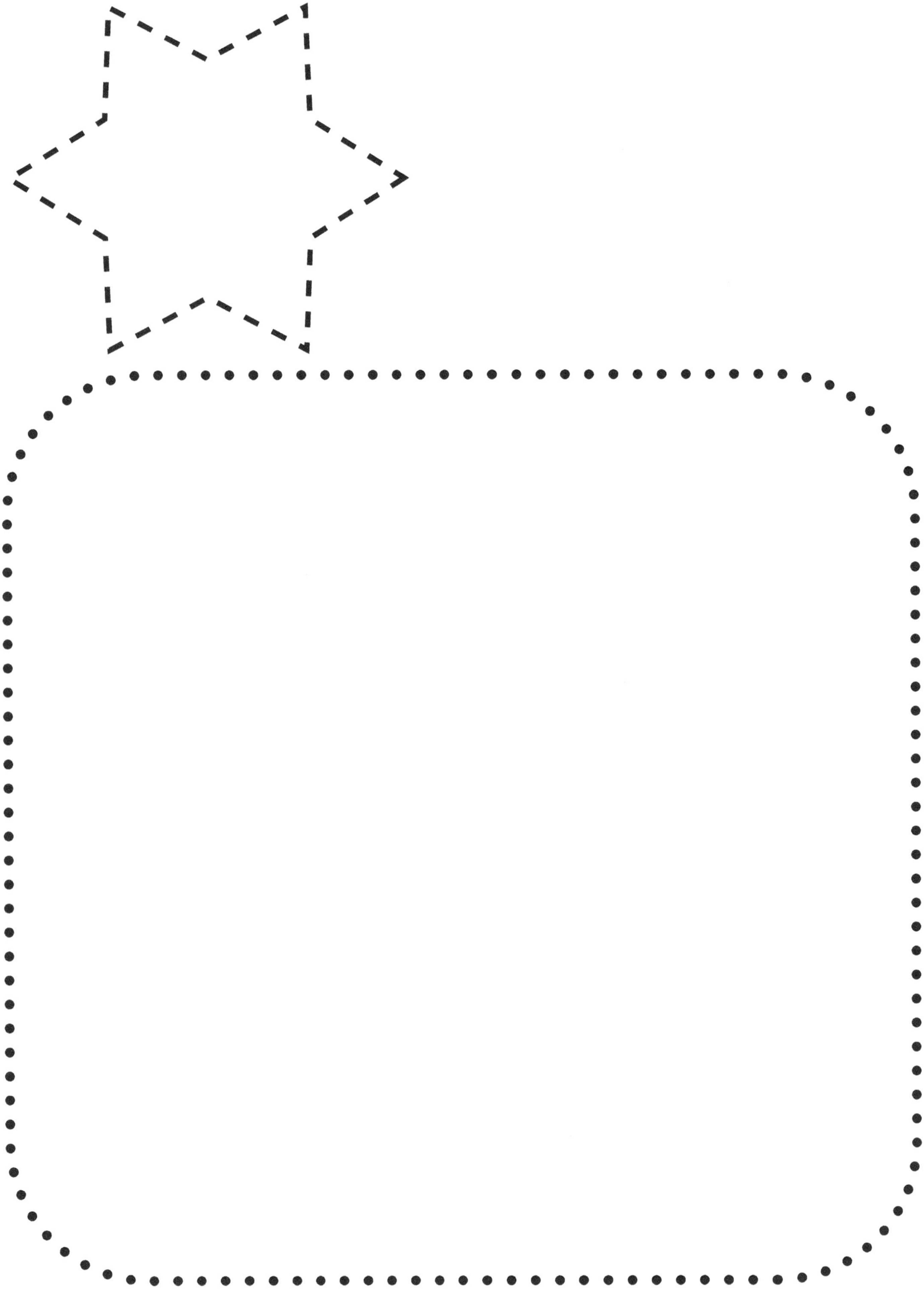

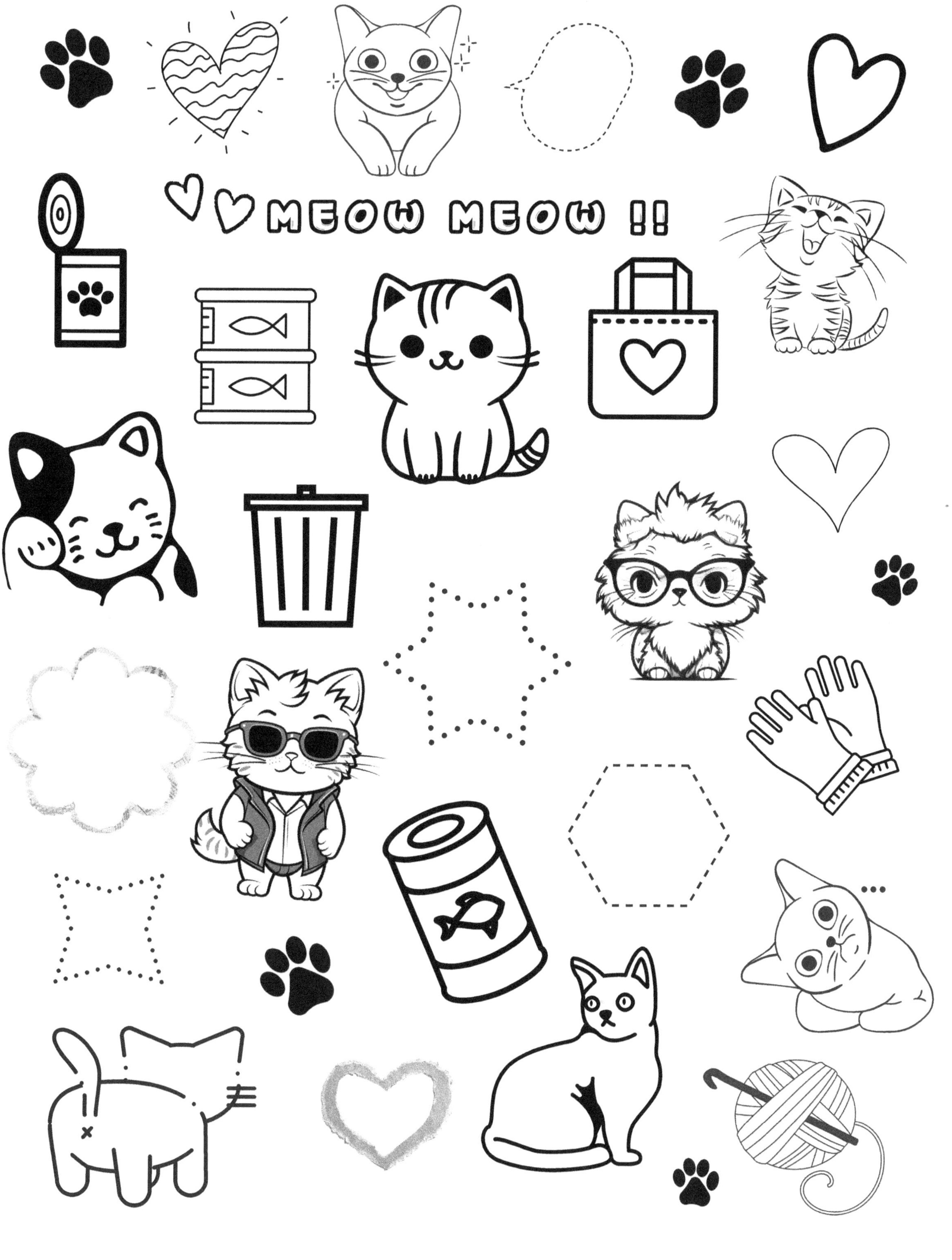
MEOW MEOW !!

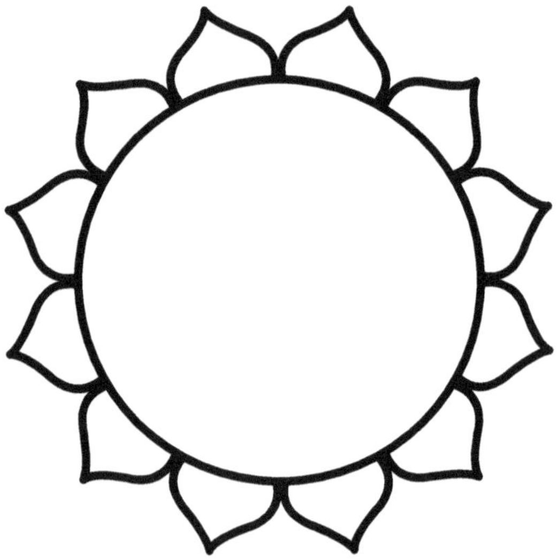

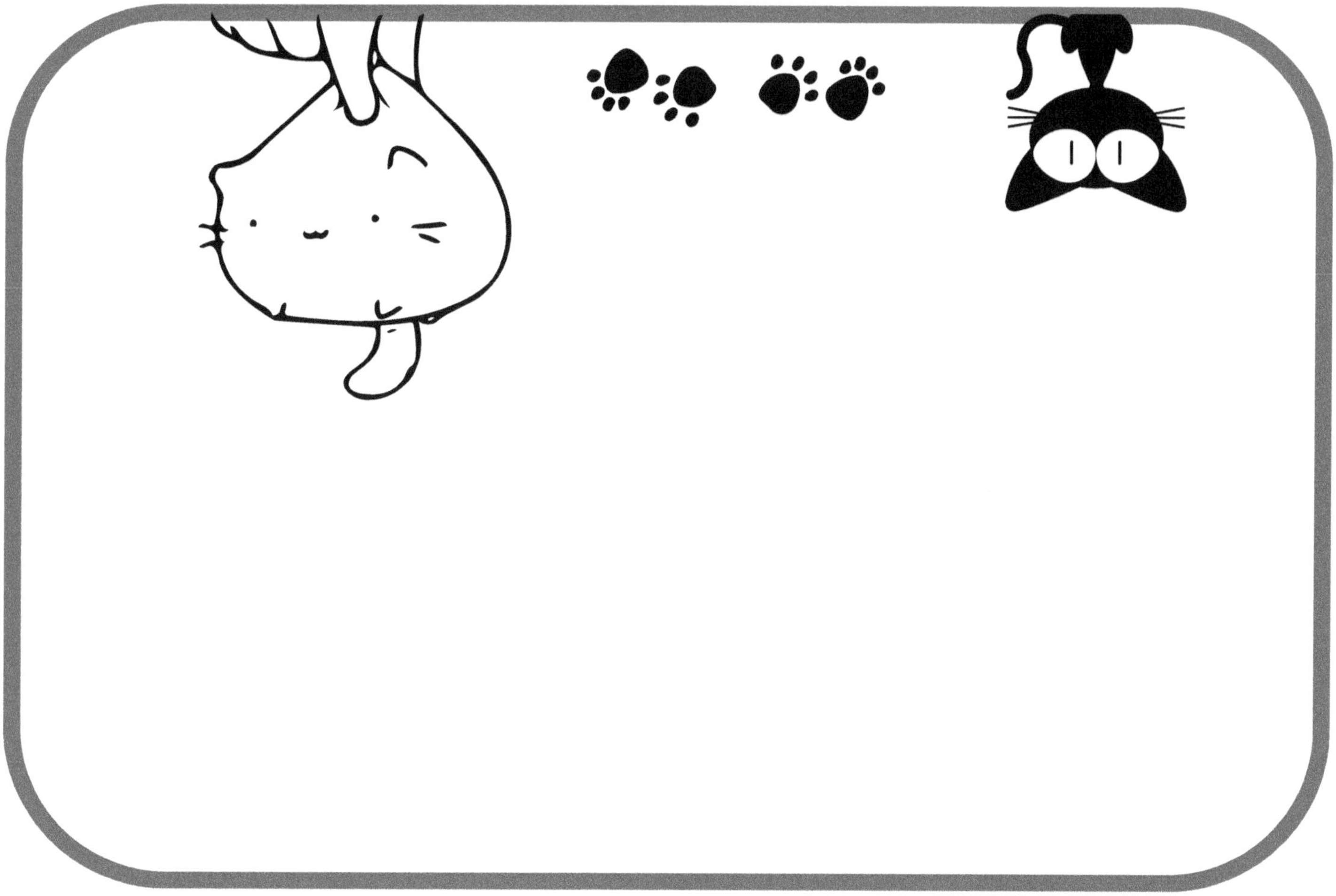

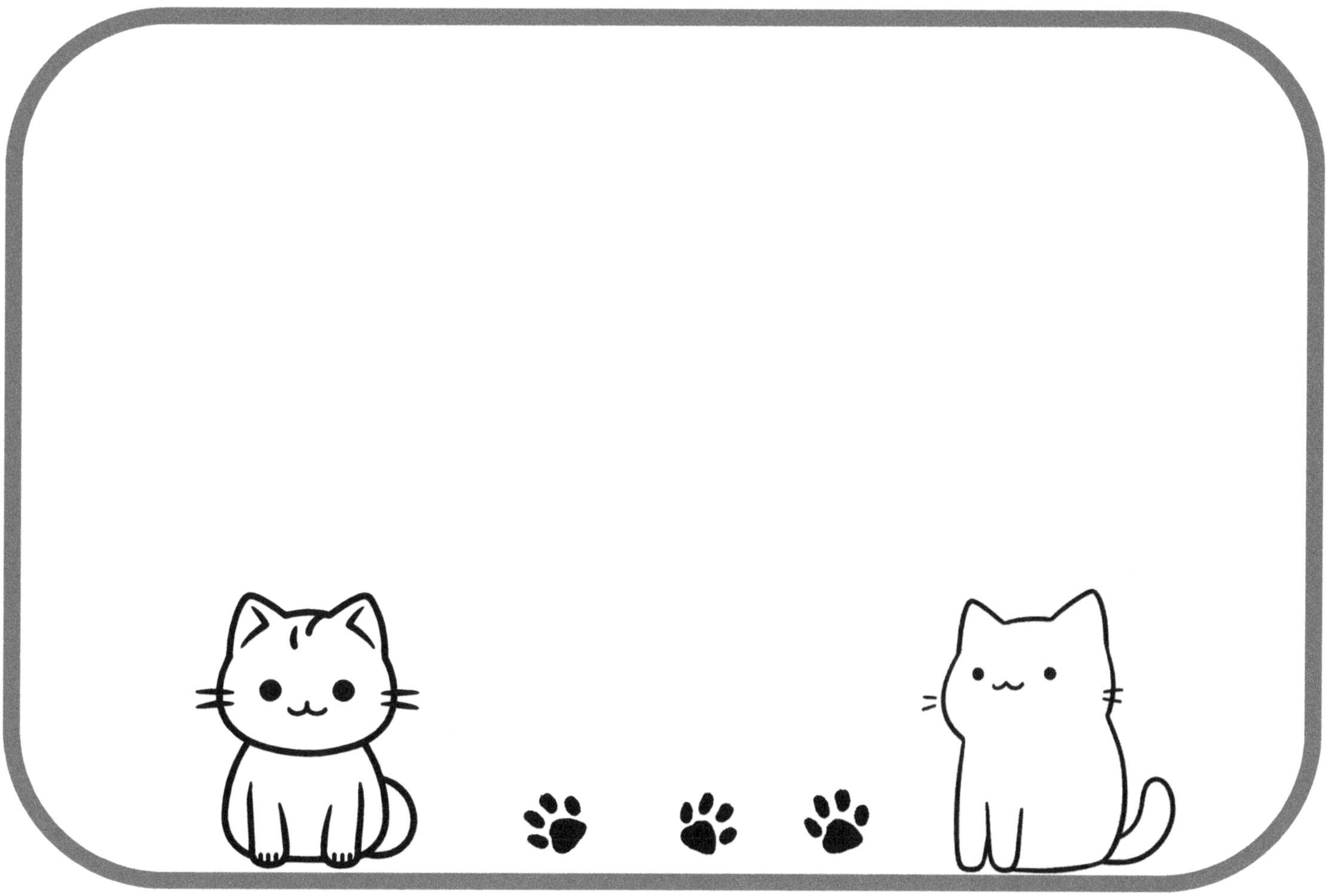

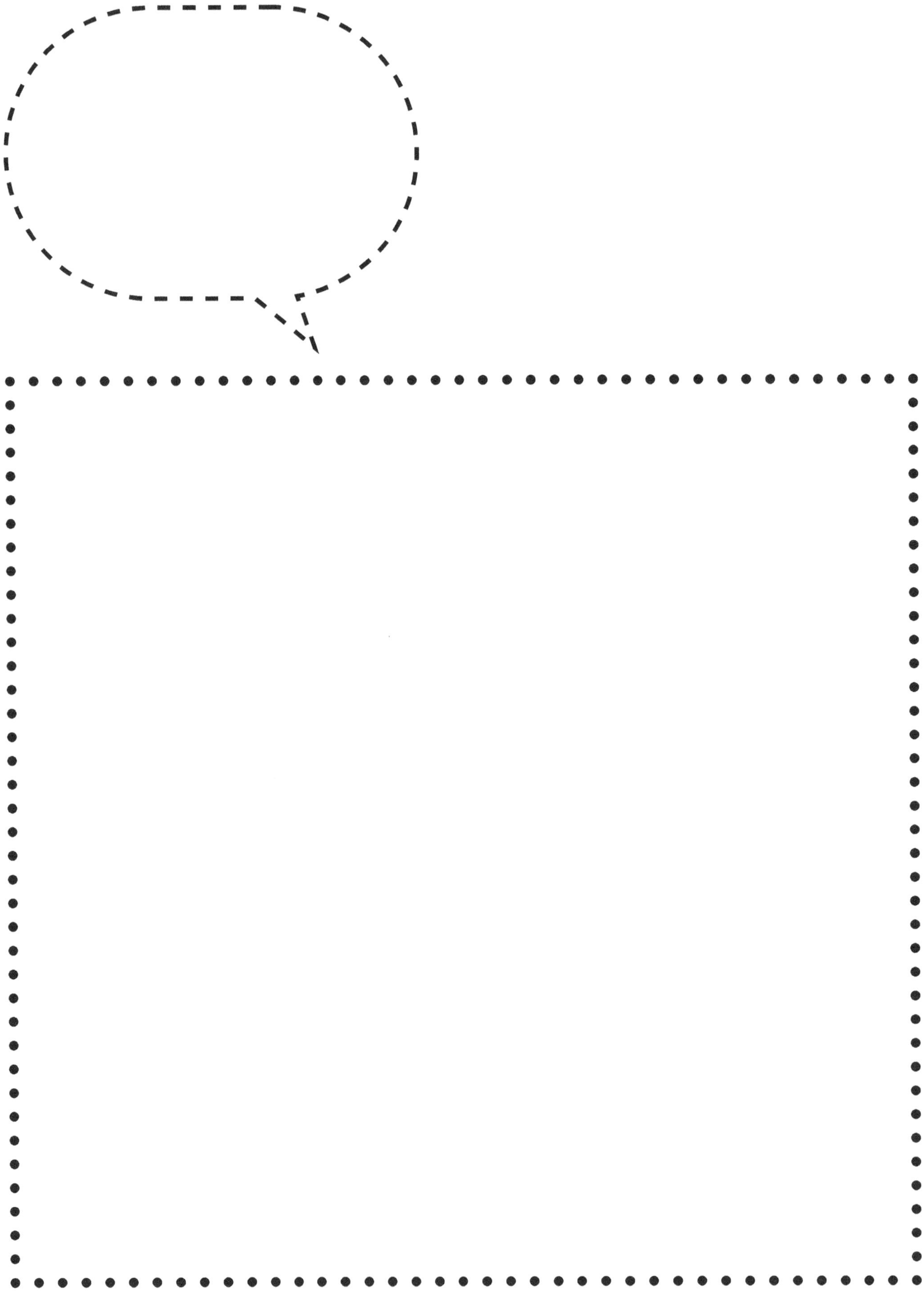

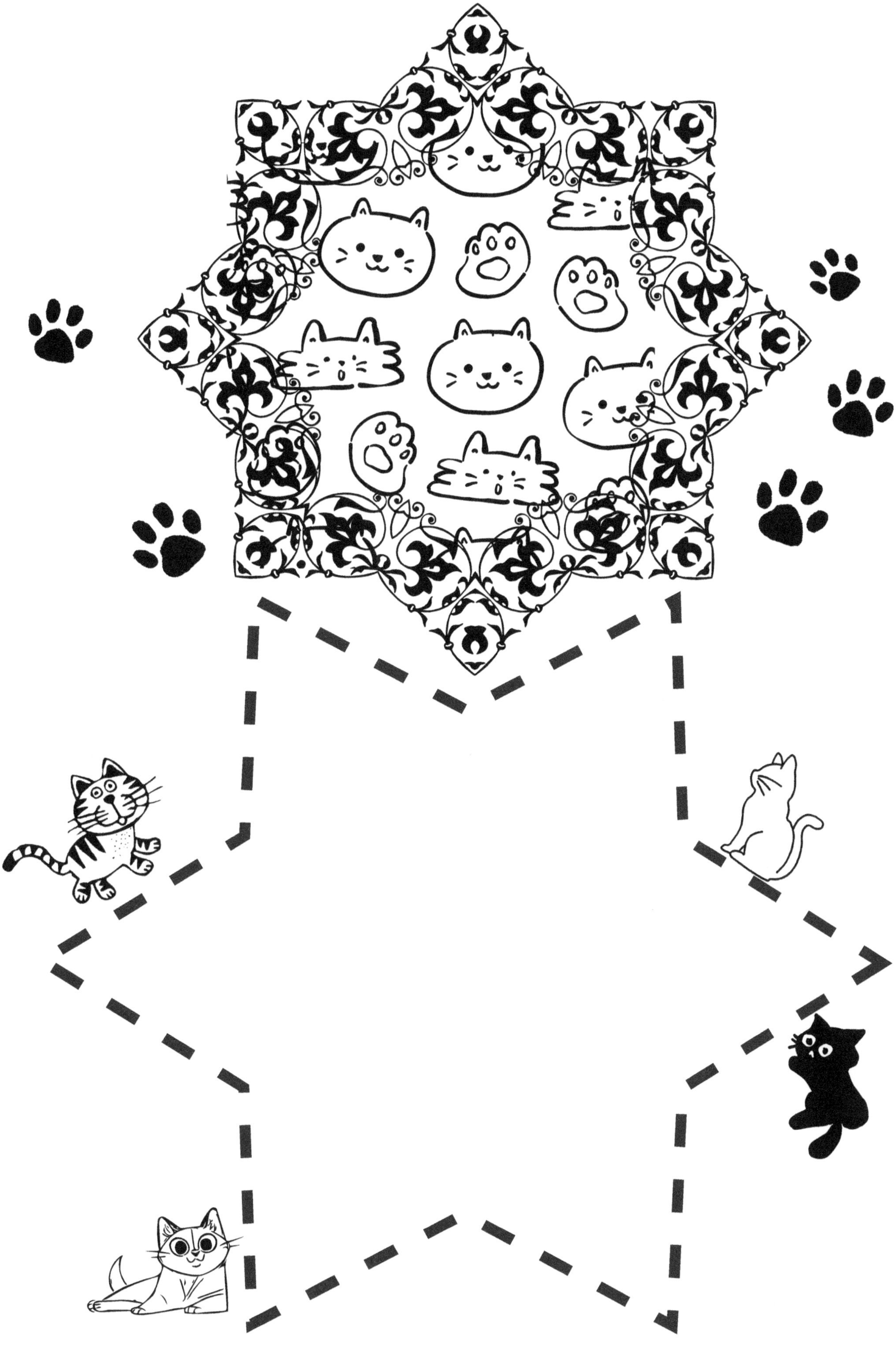

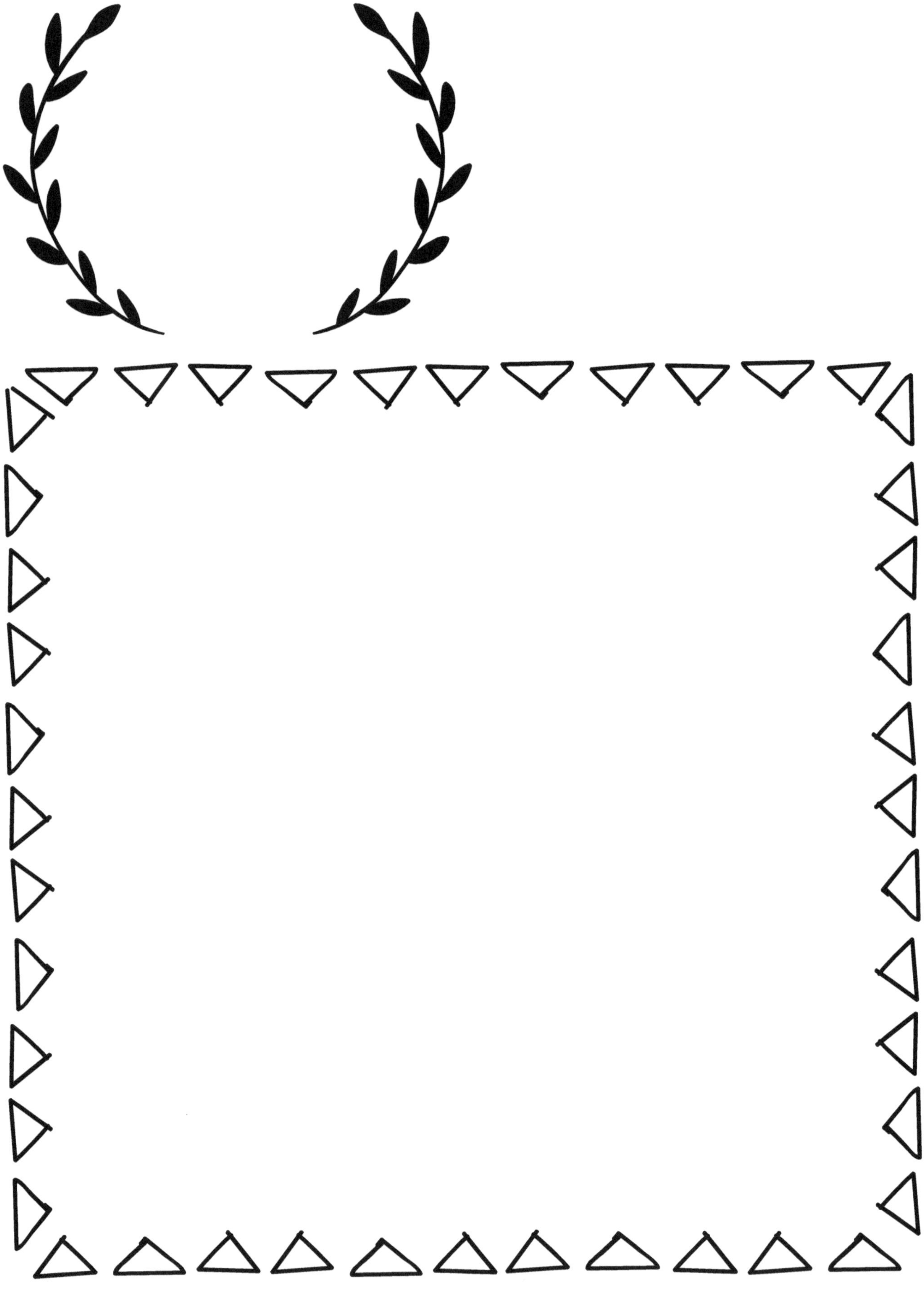

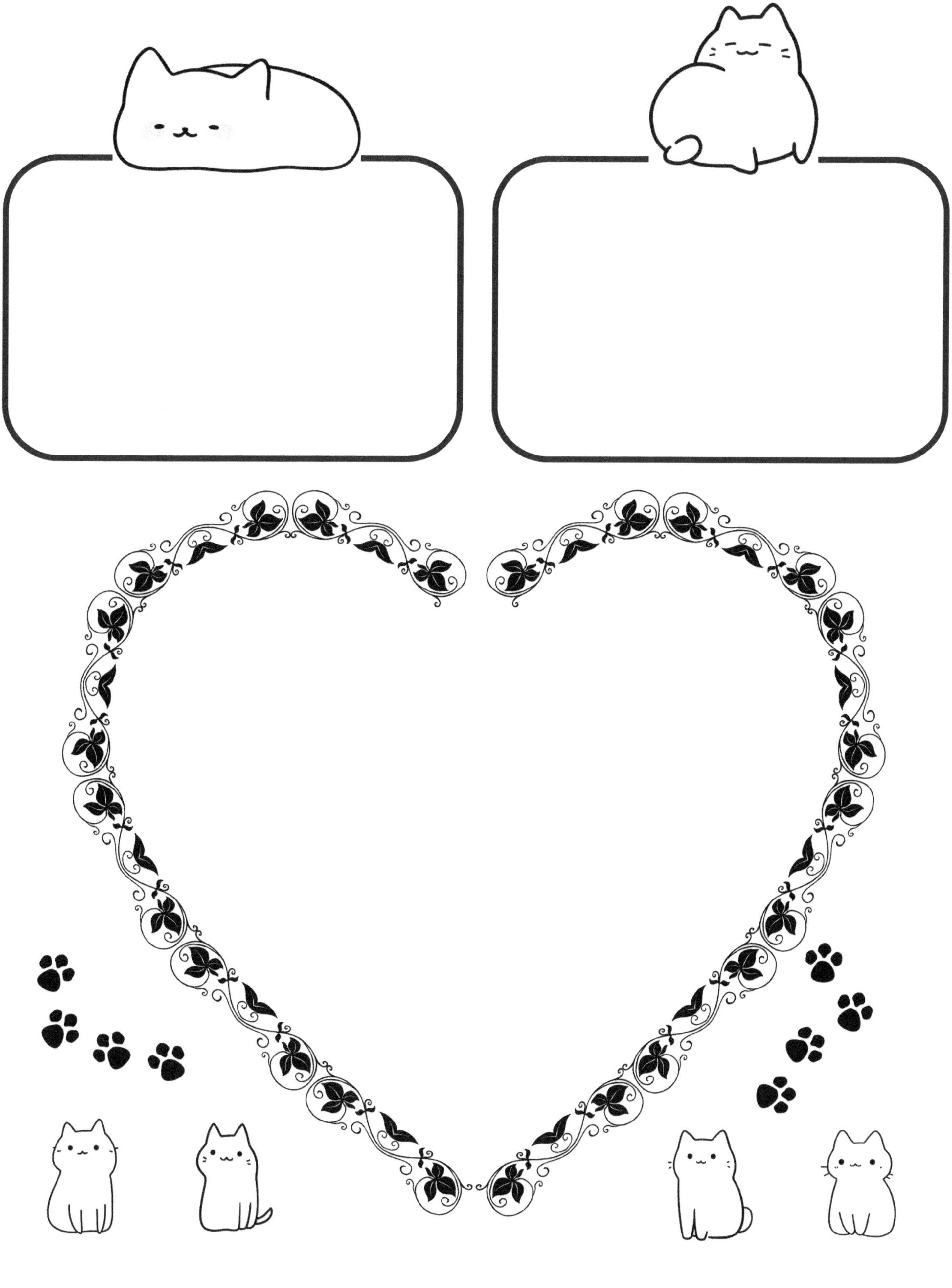

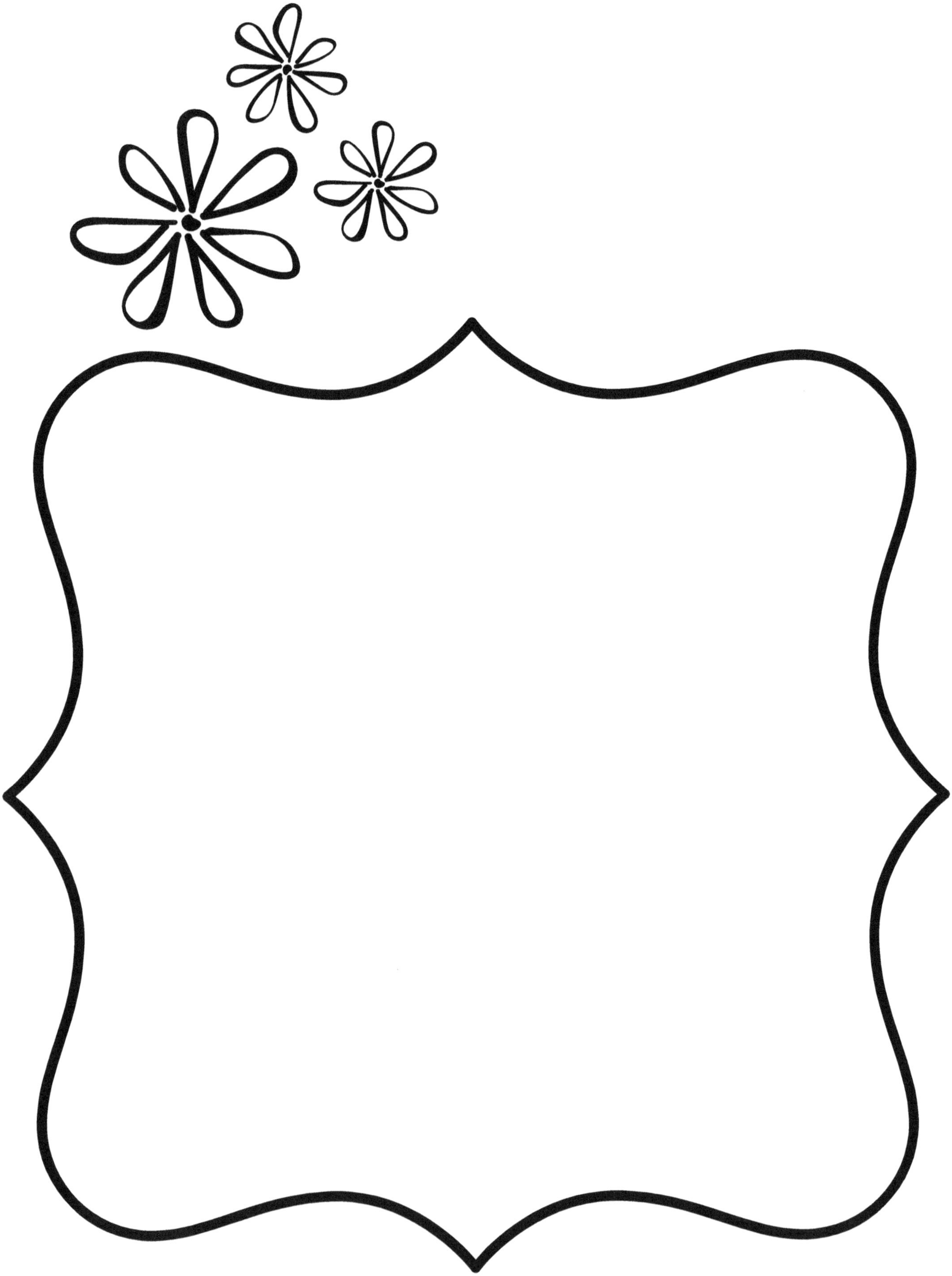

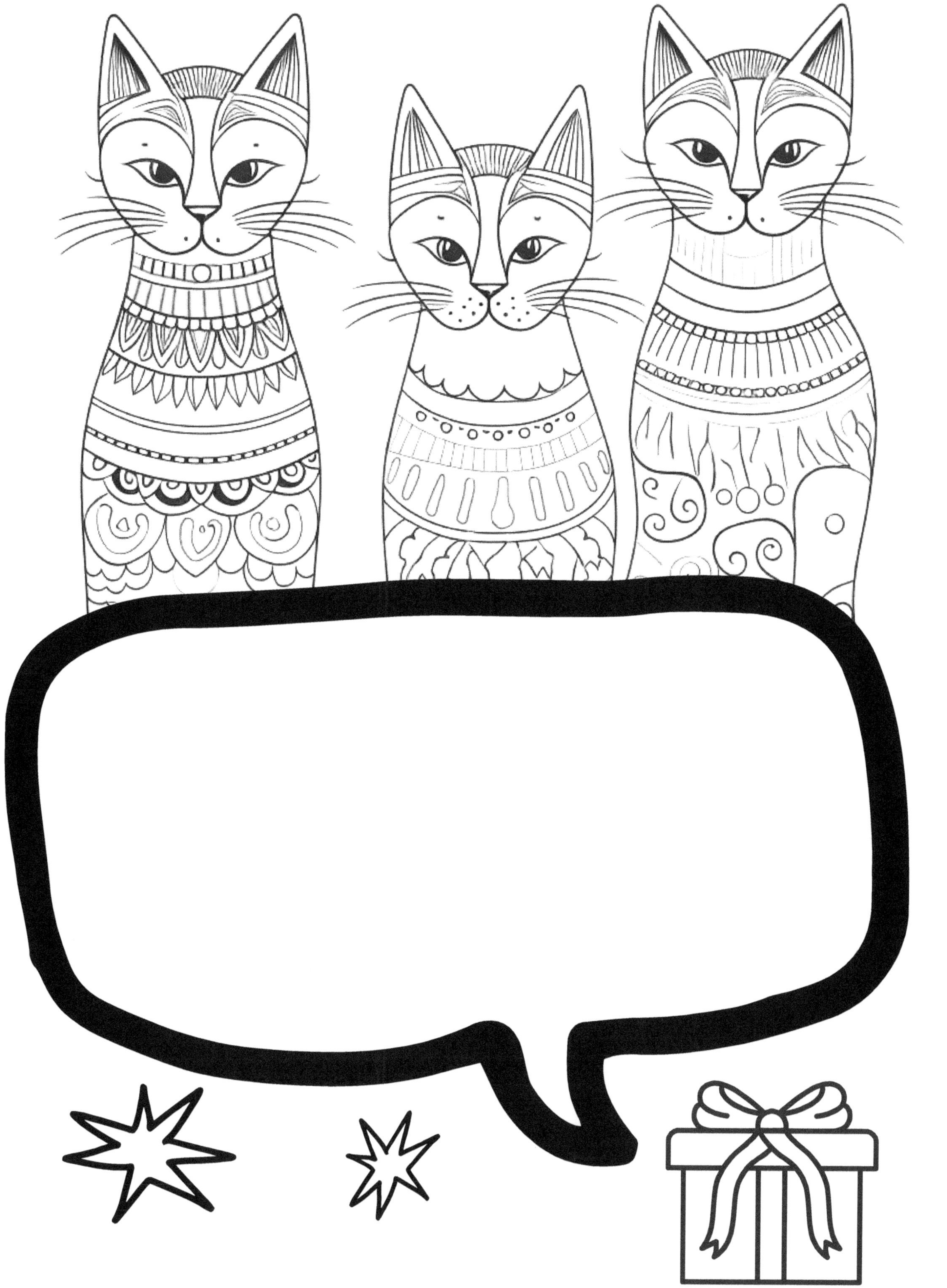

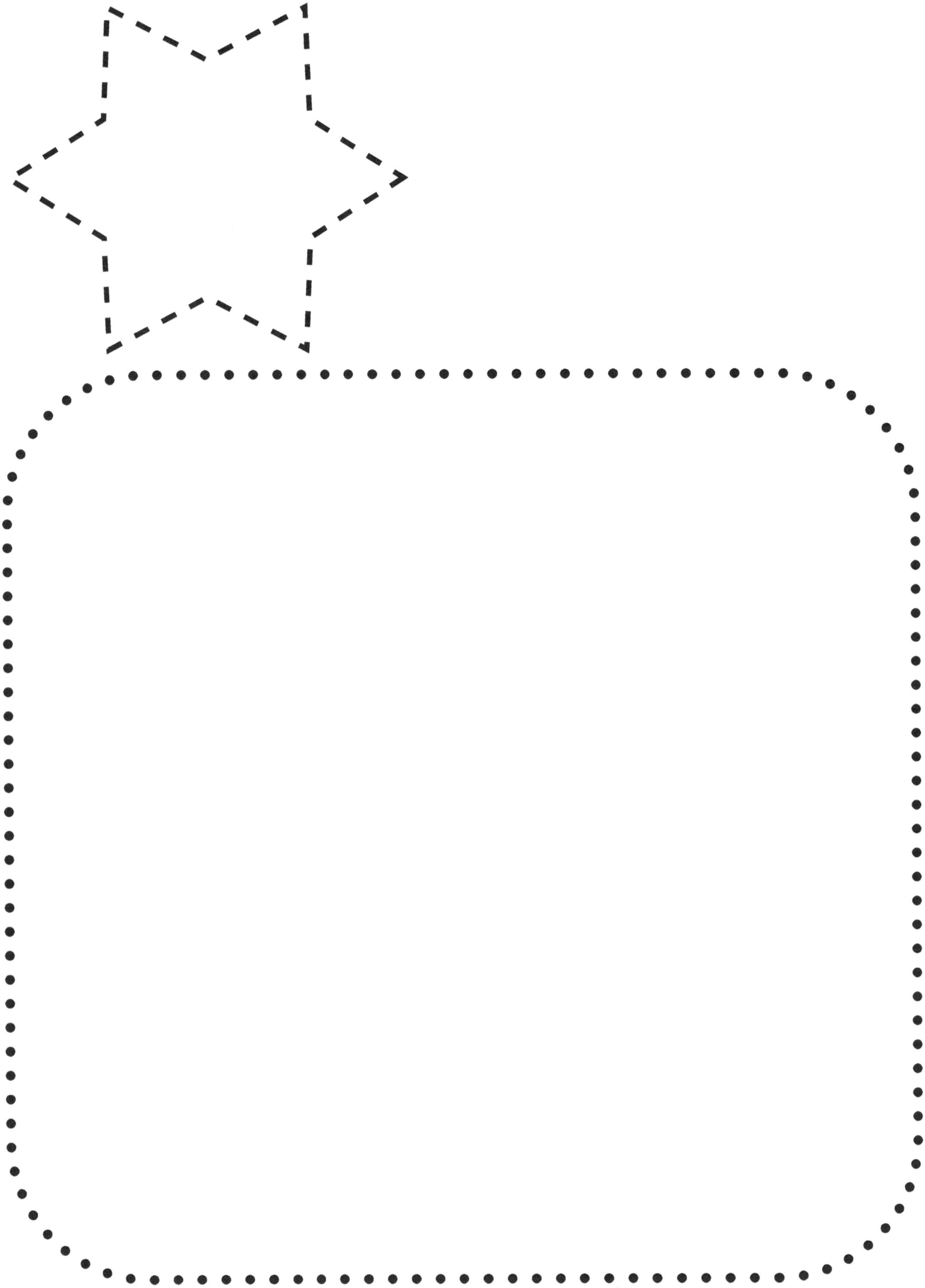

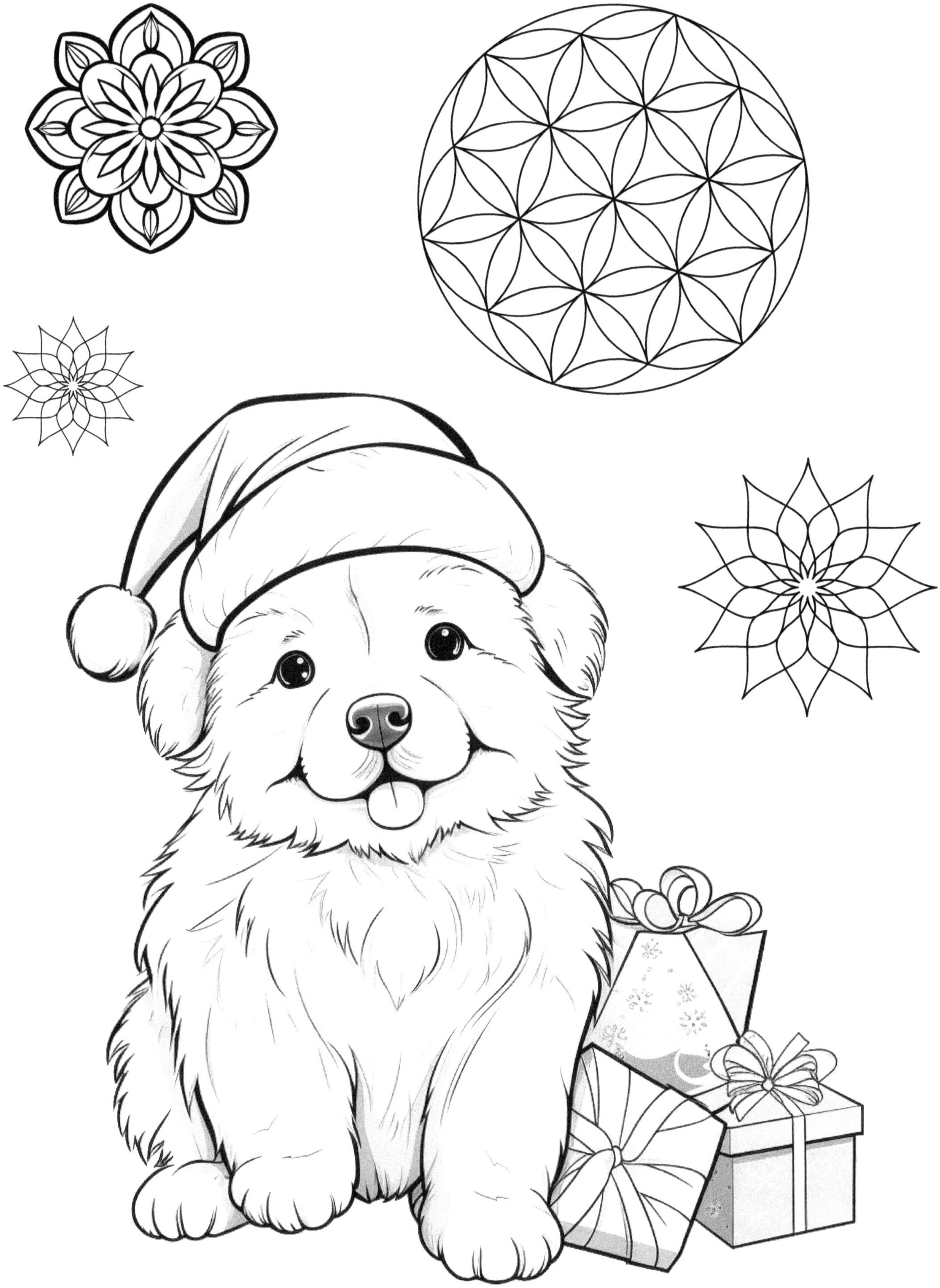

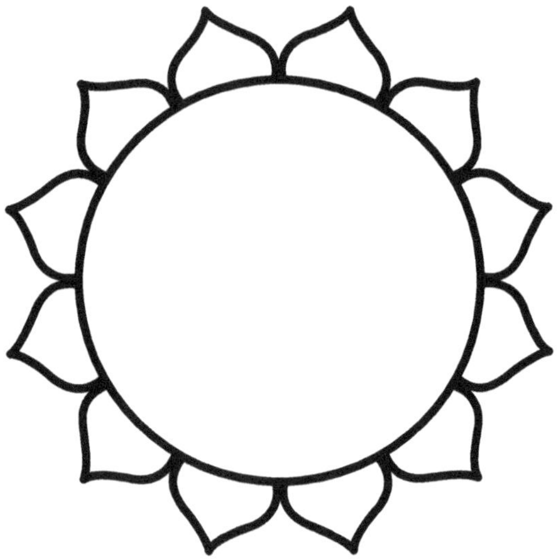

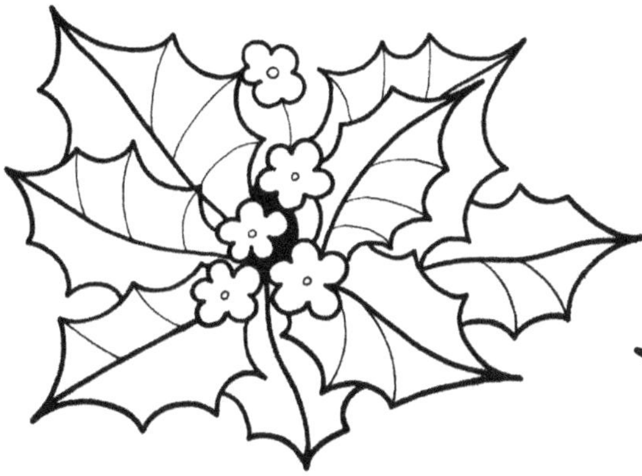

merry christmas

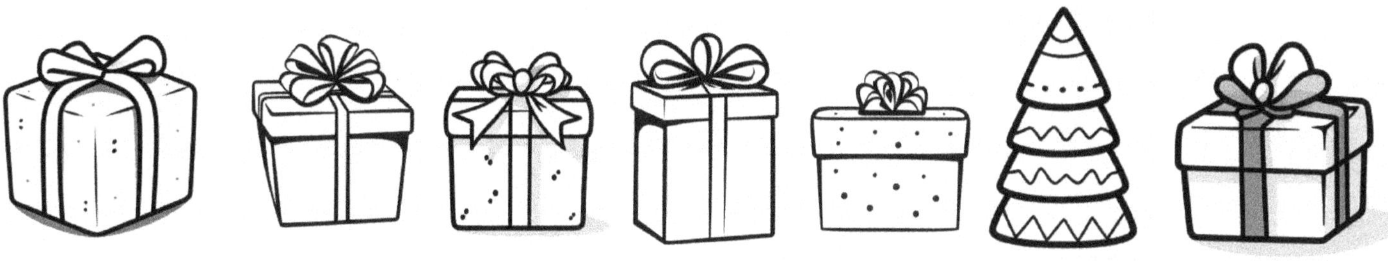

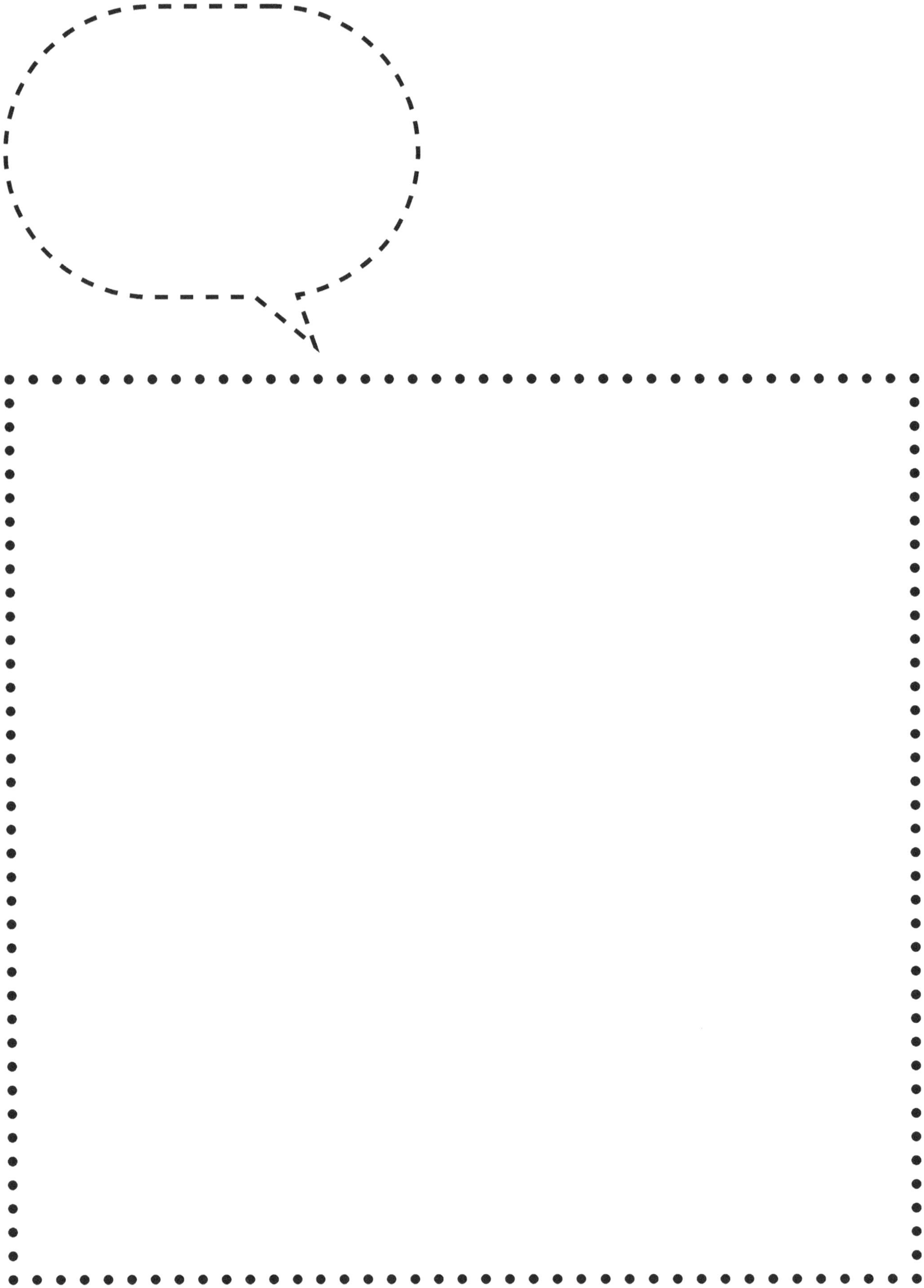

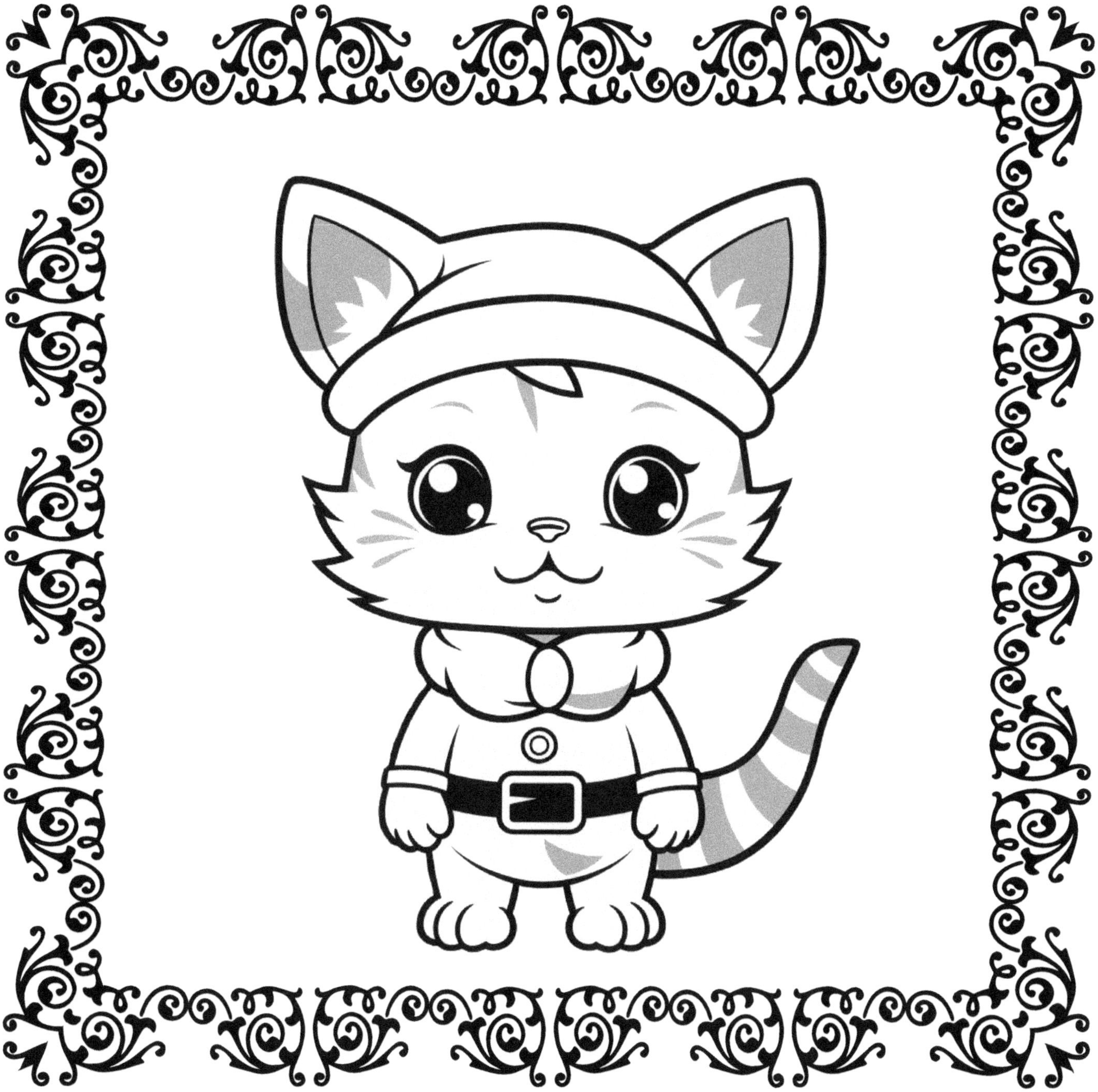

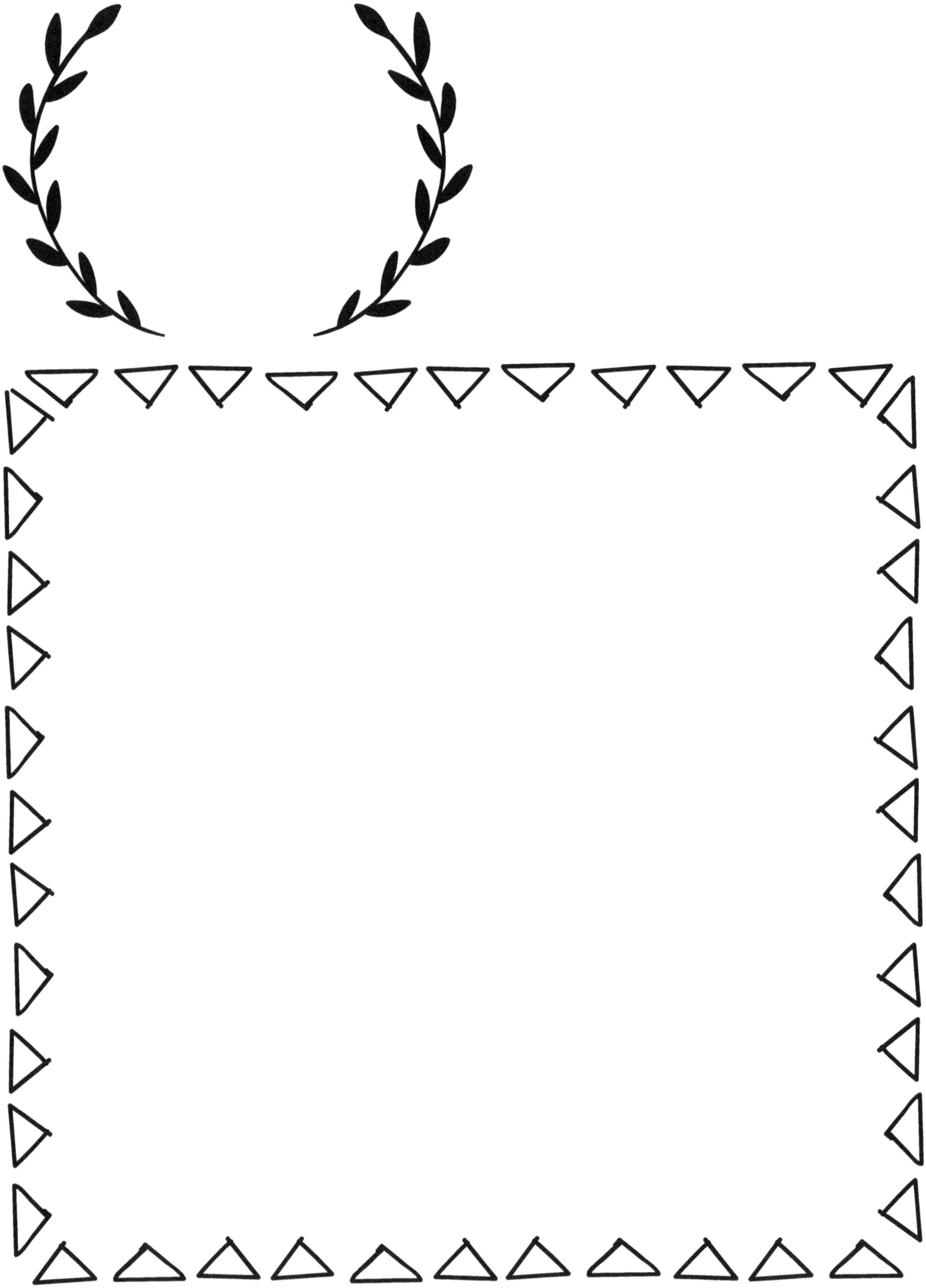

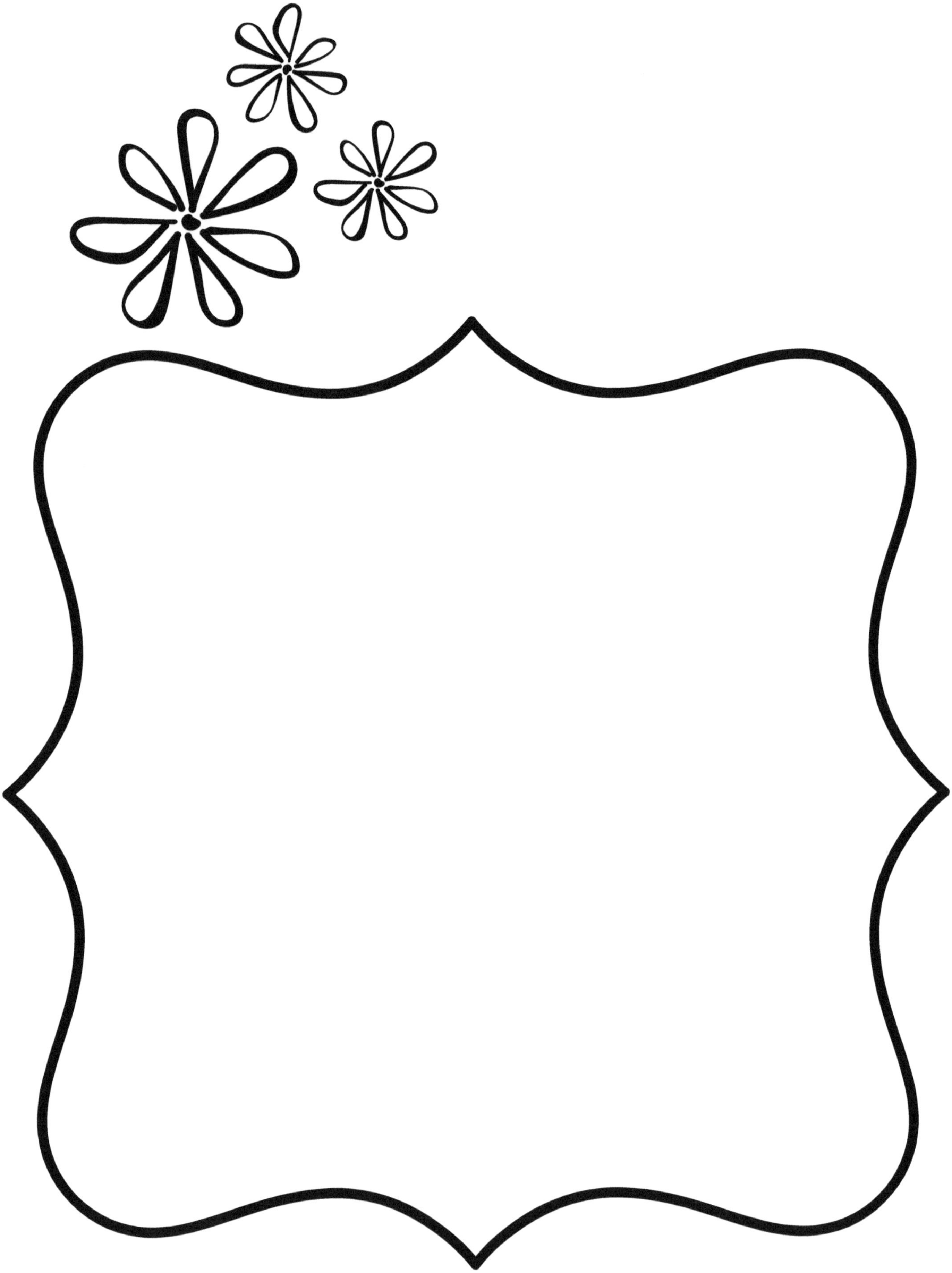

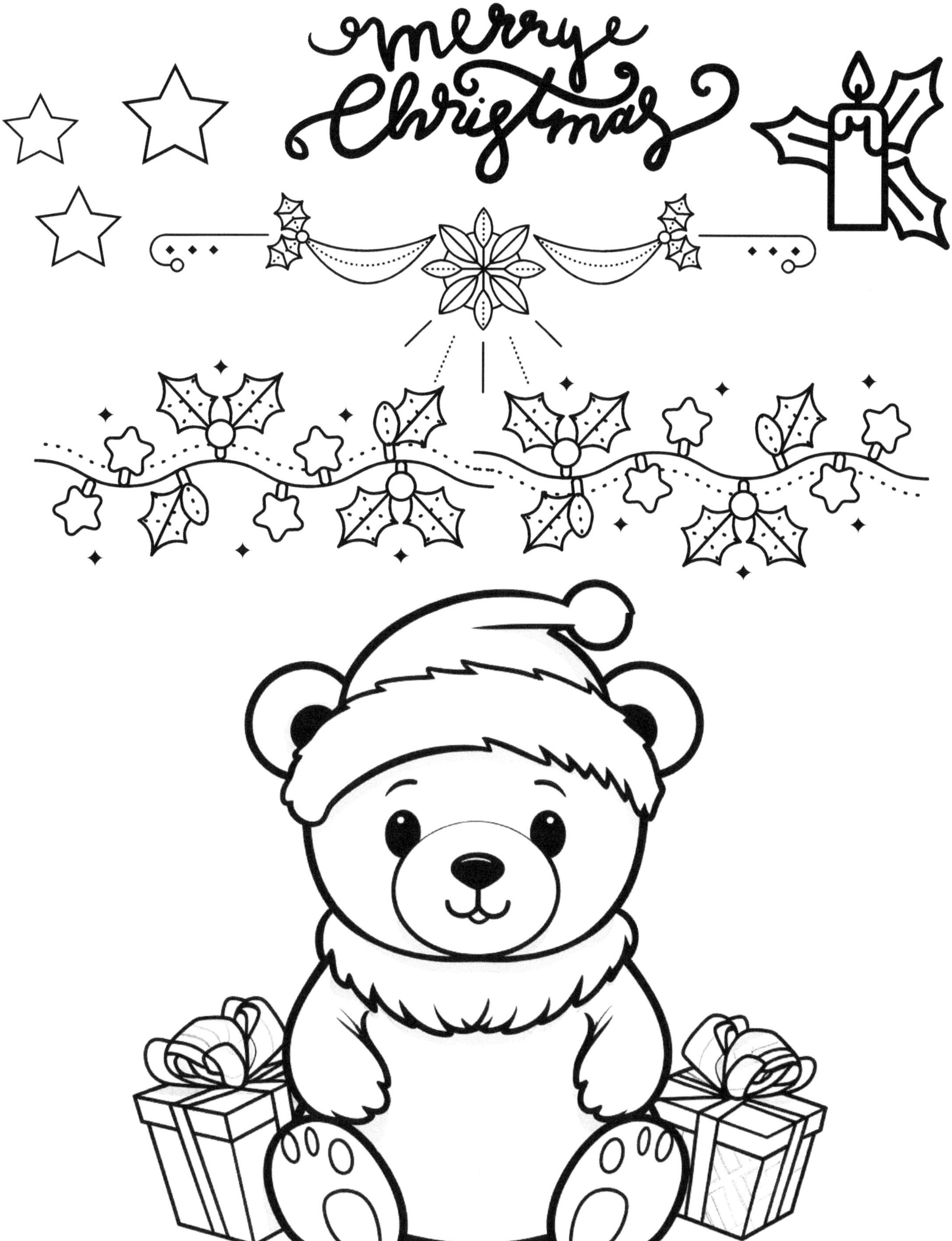
Merry Christmas

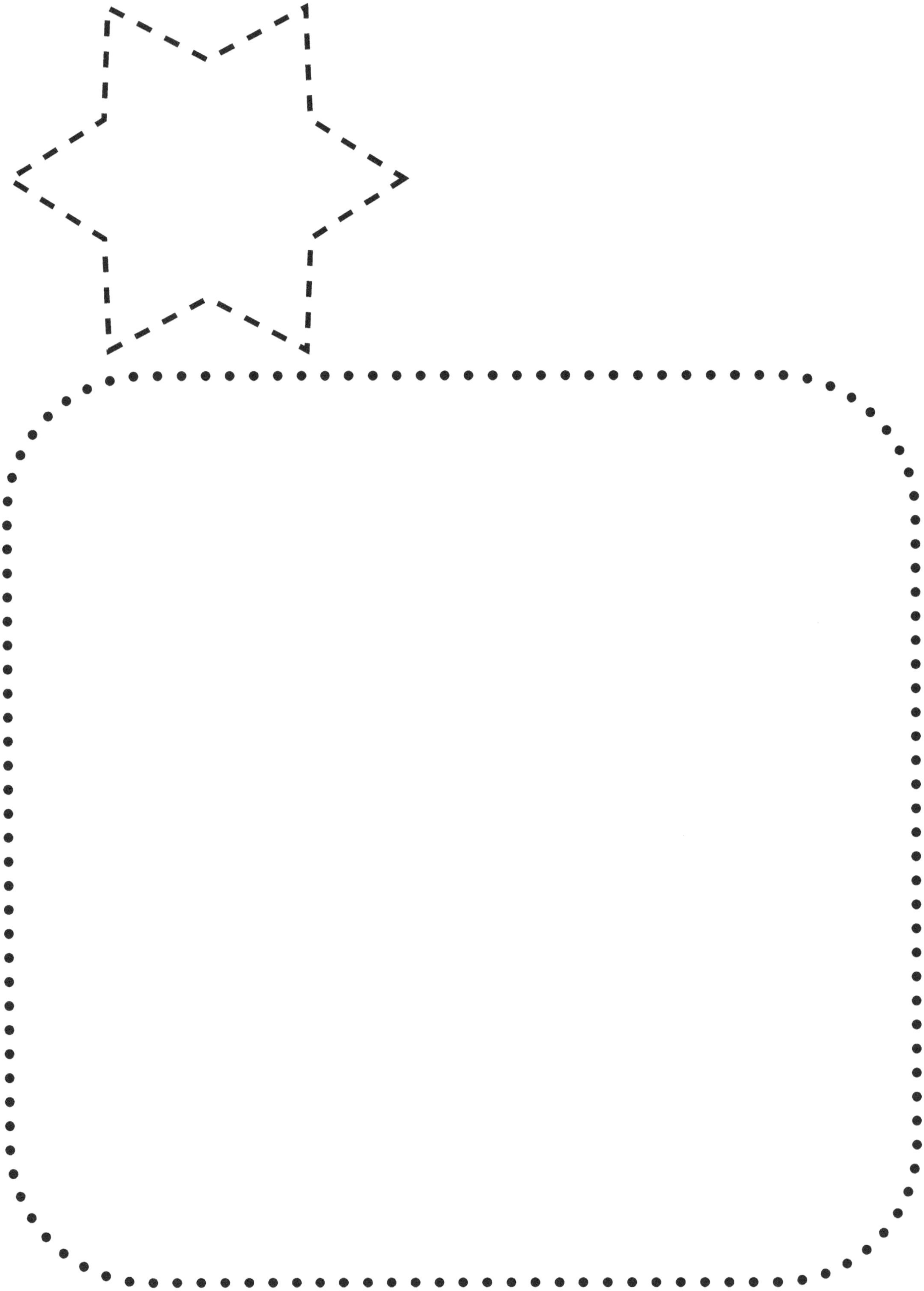

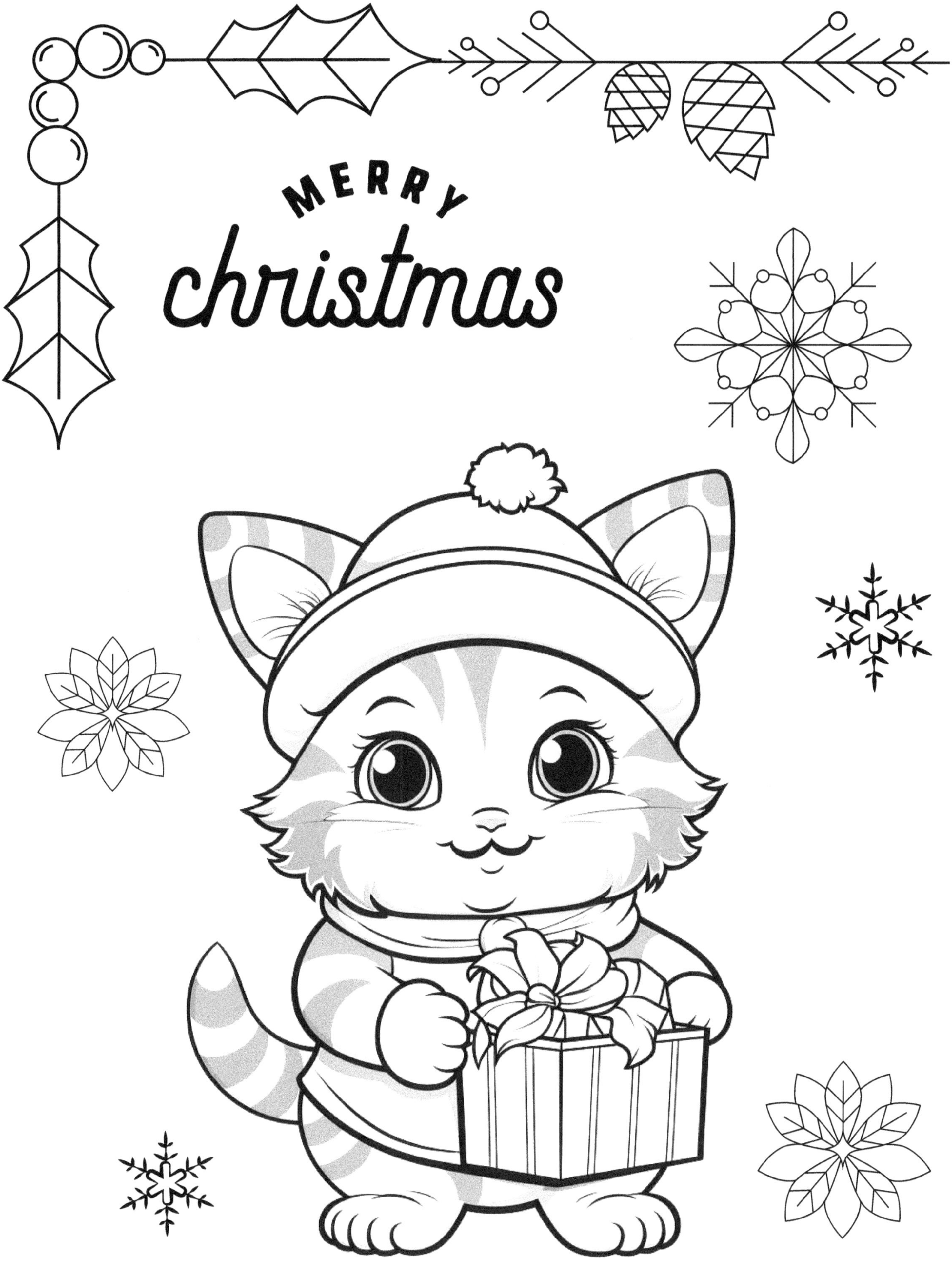
MERRY
christmas

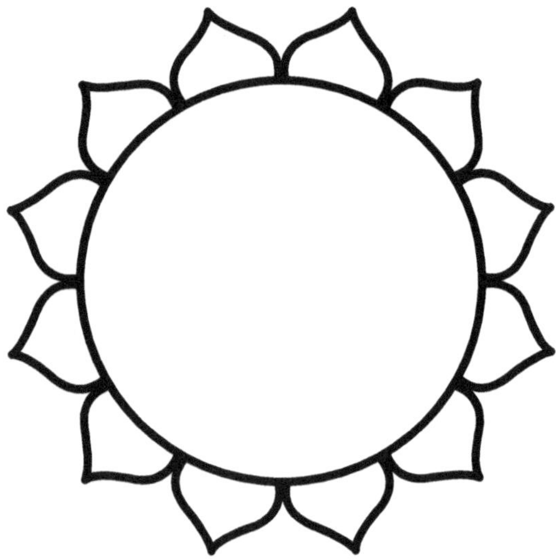

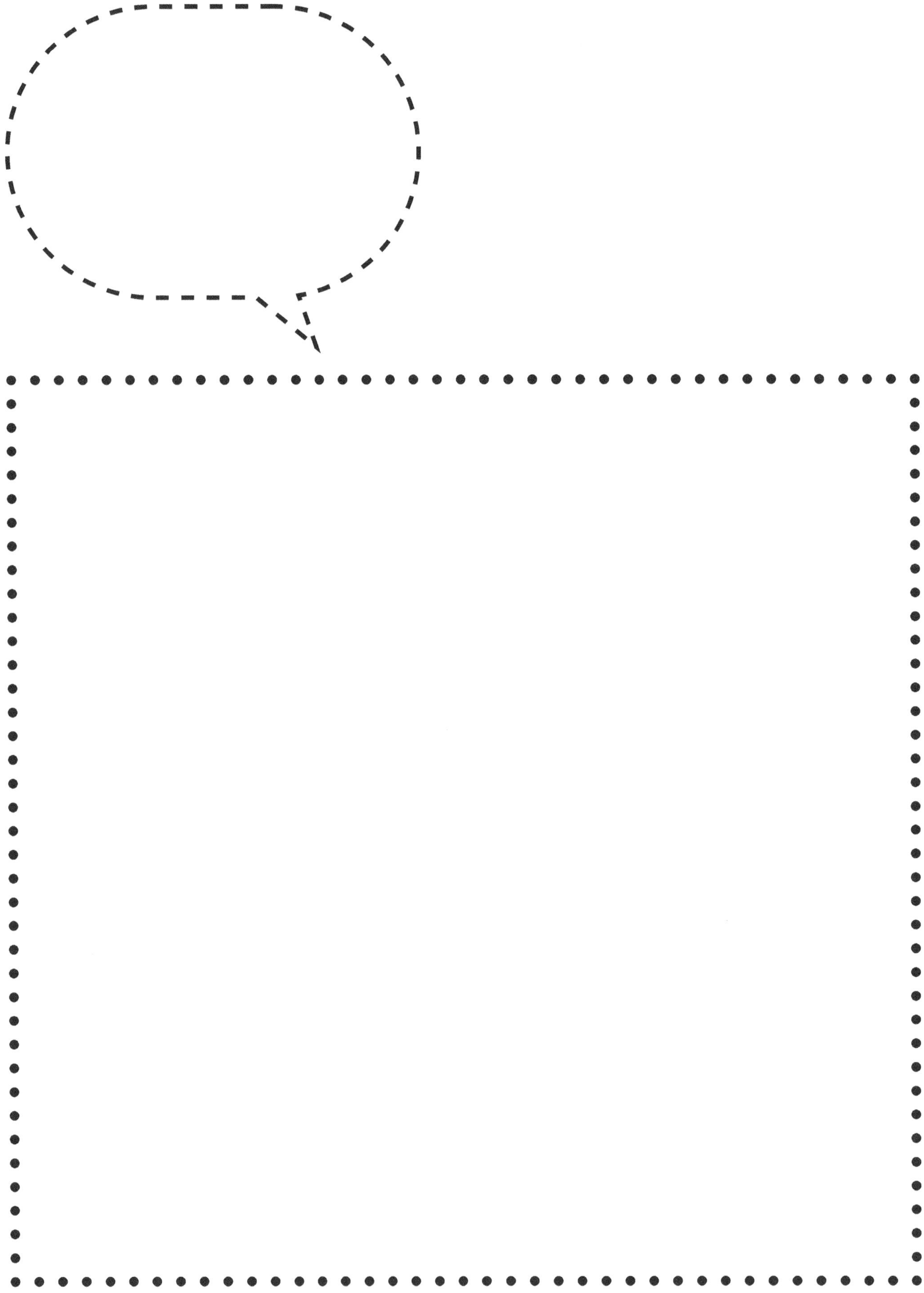

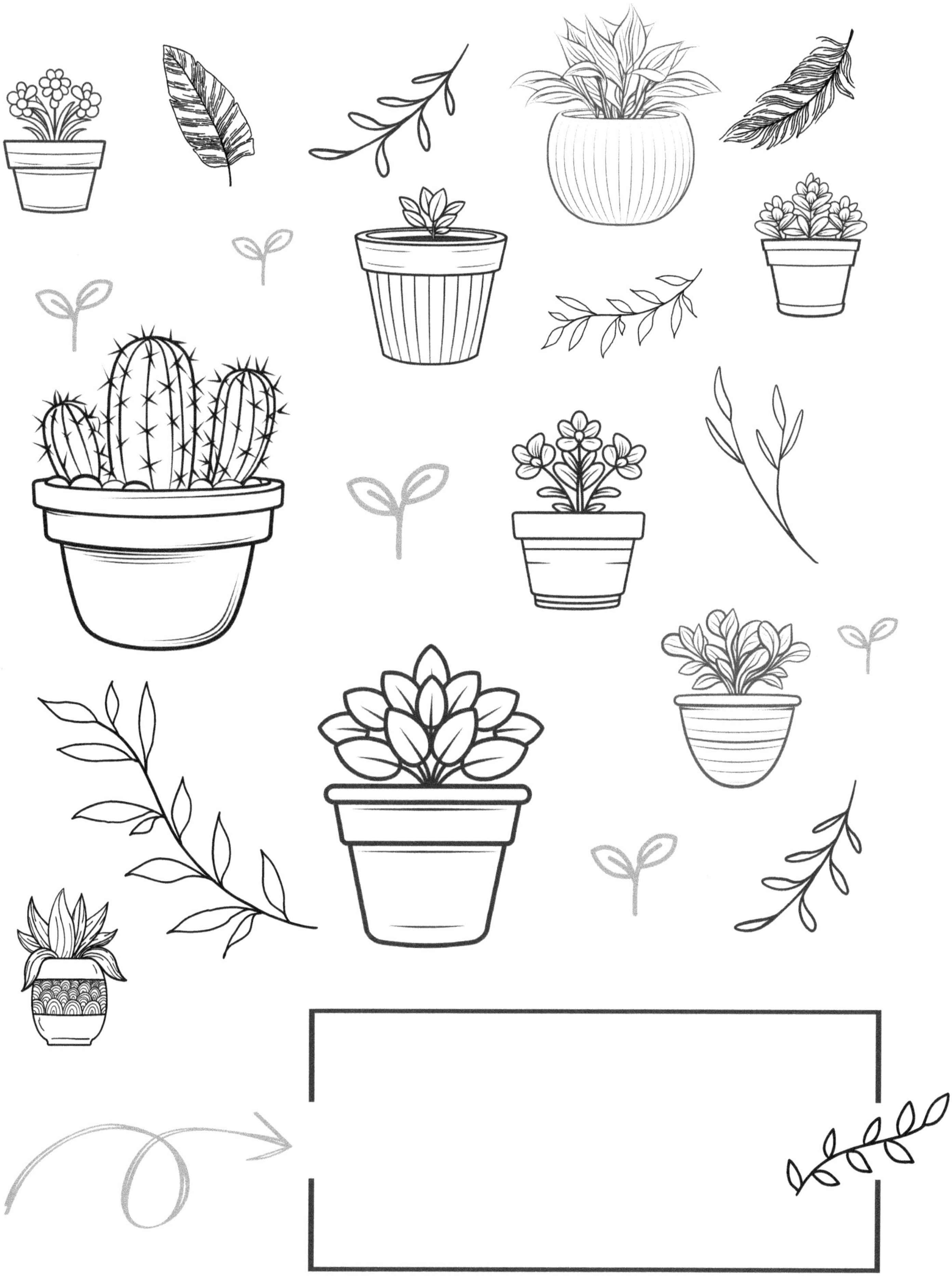

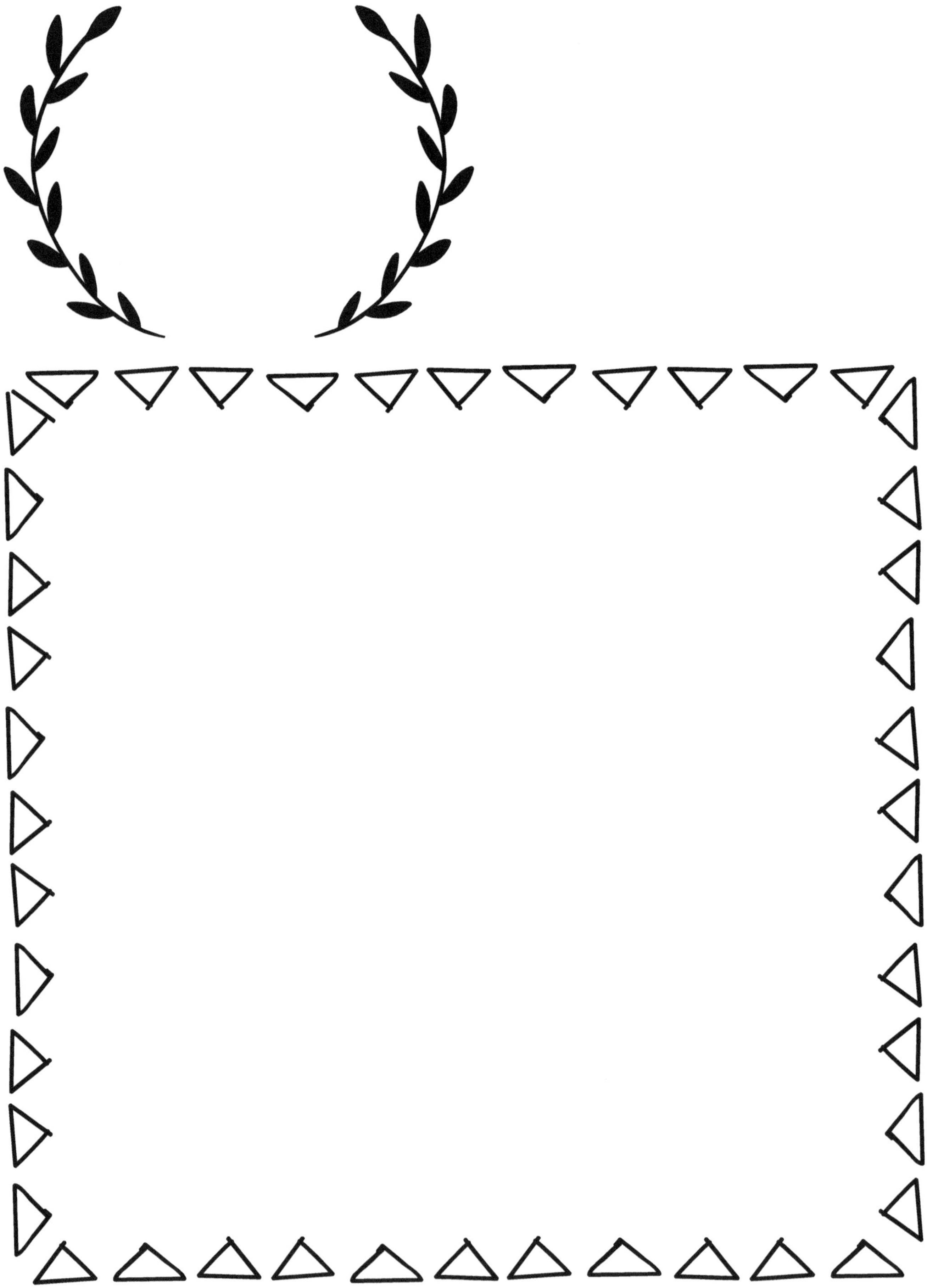

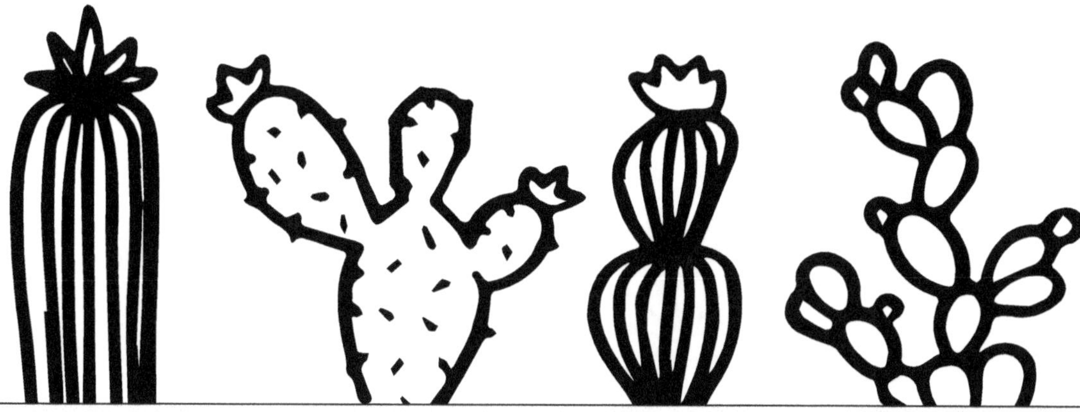

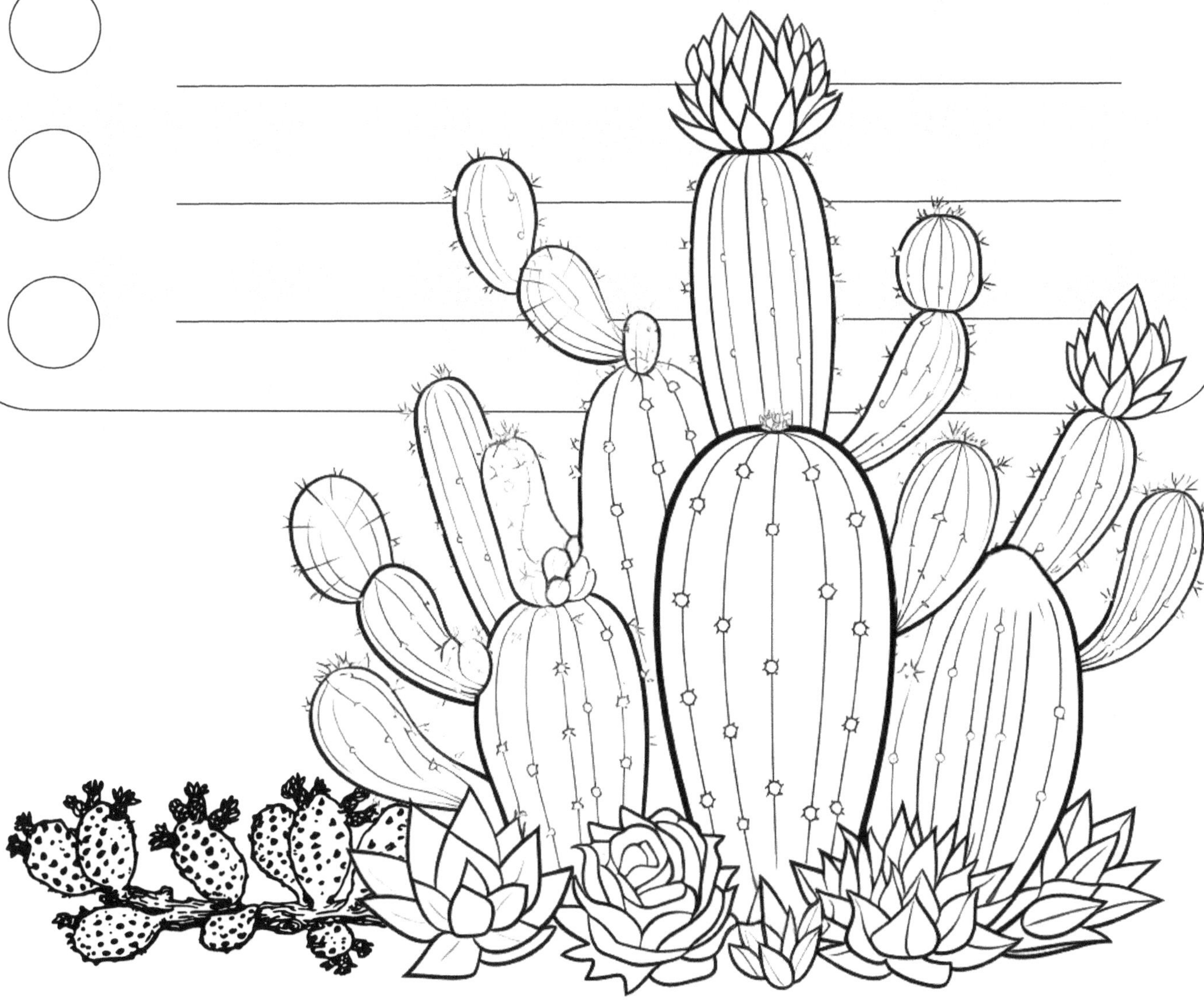

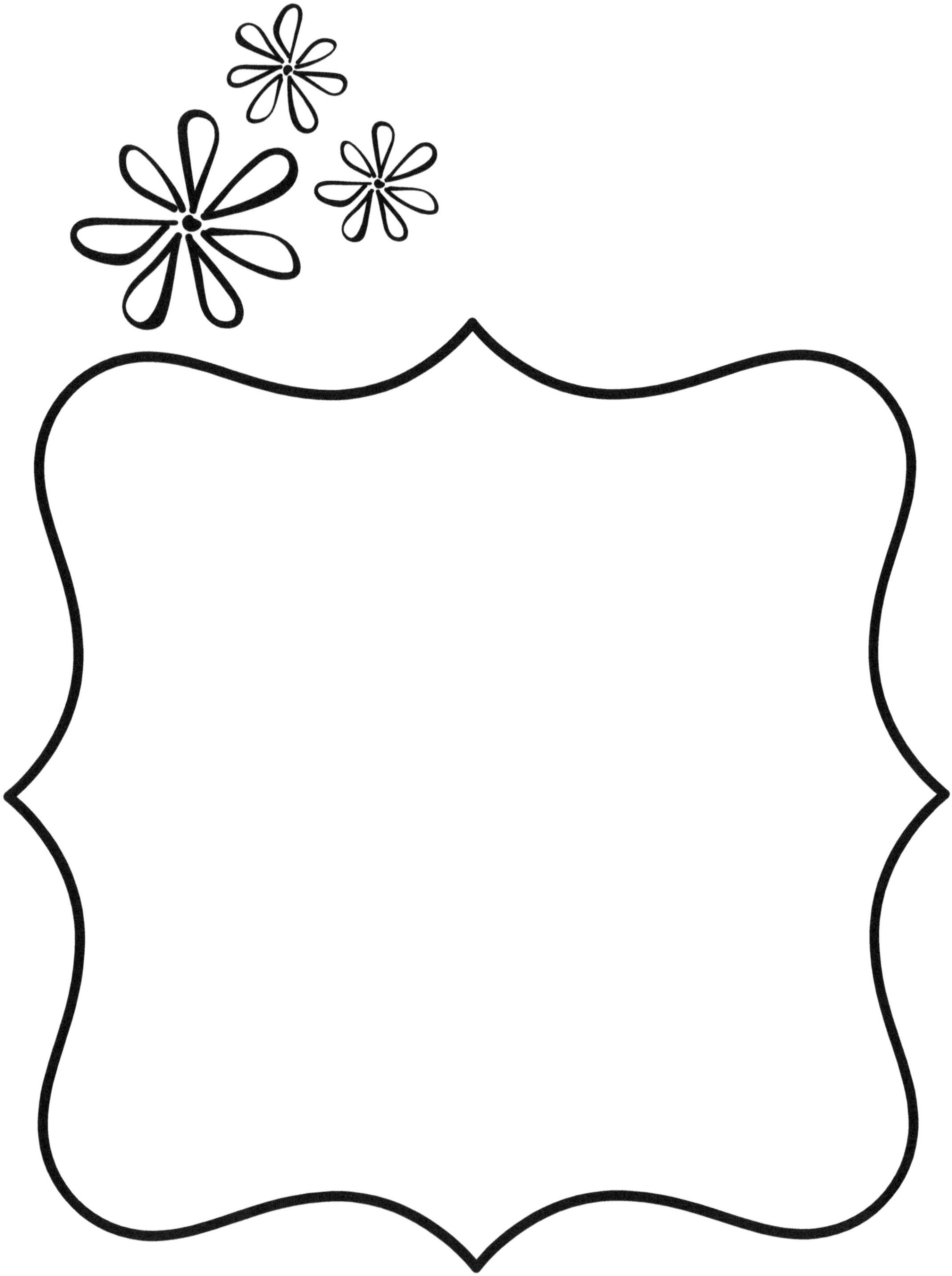

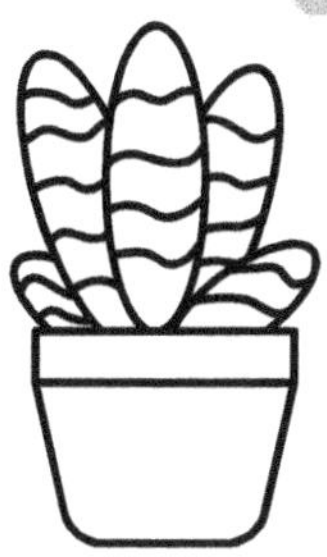

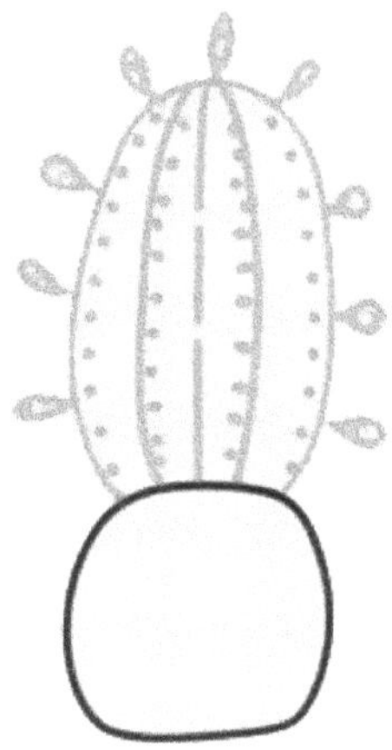

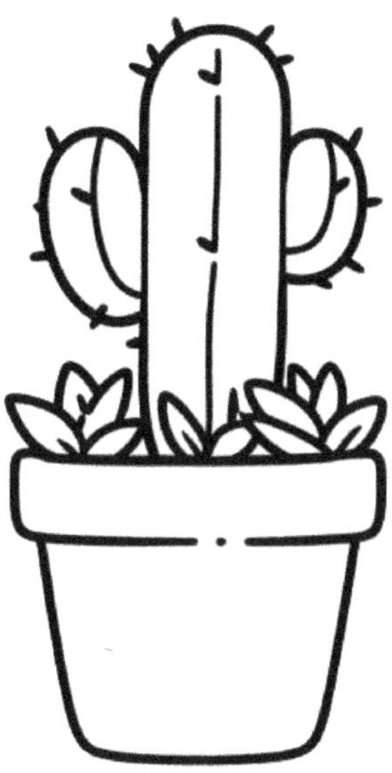

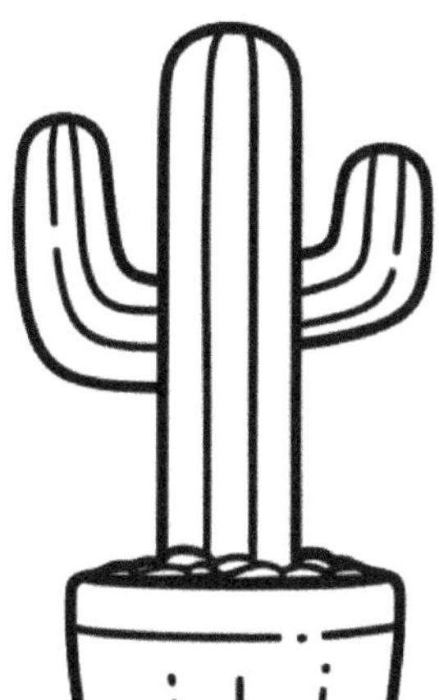

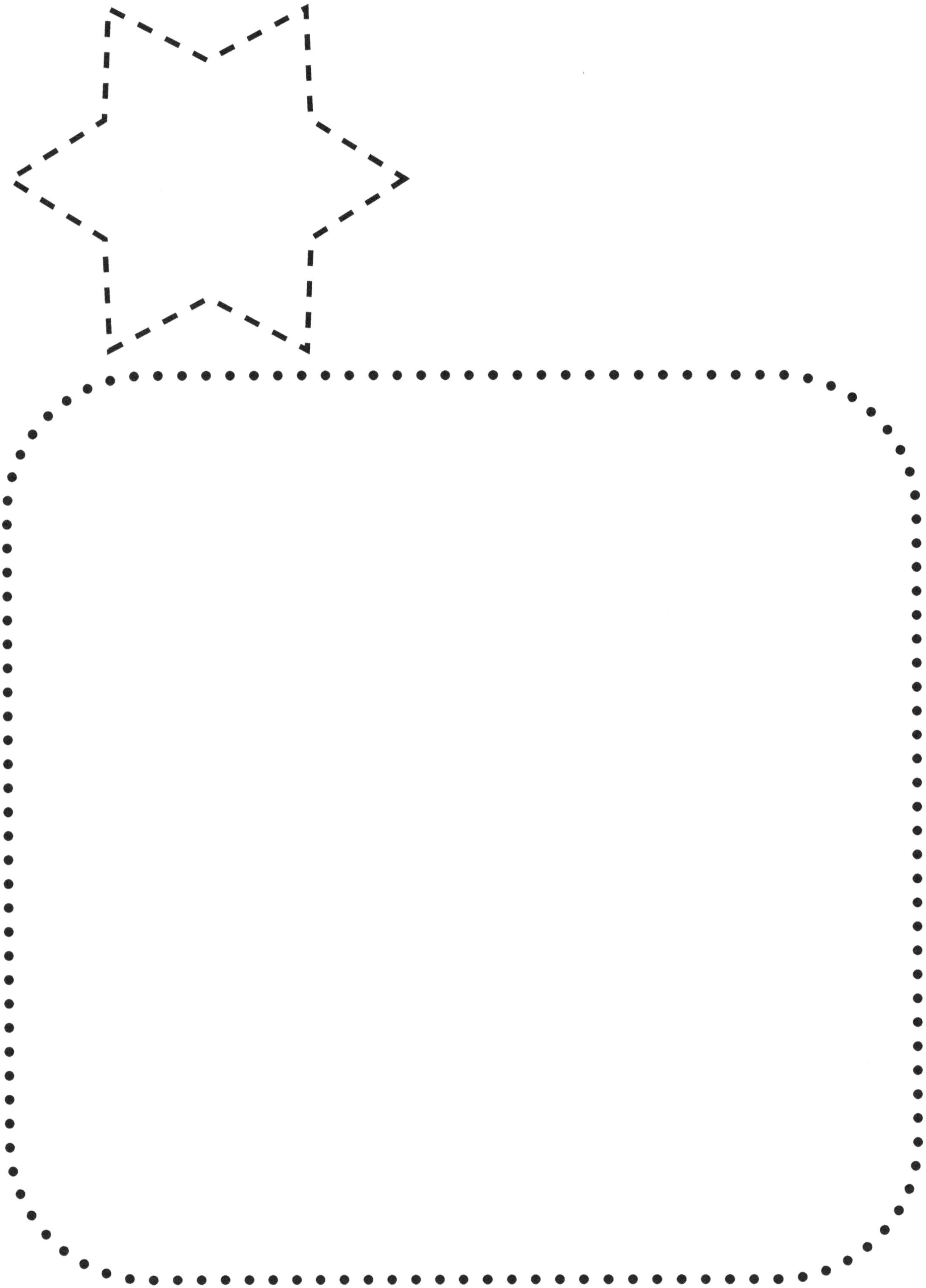

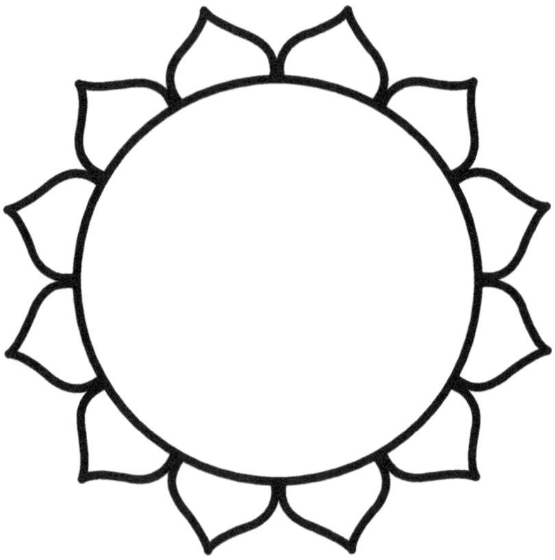

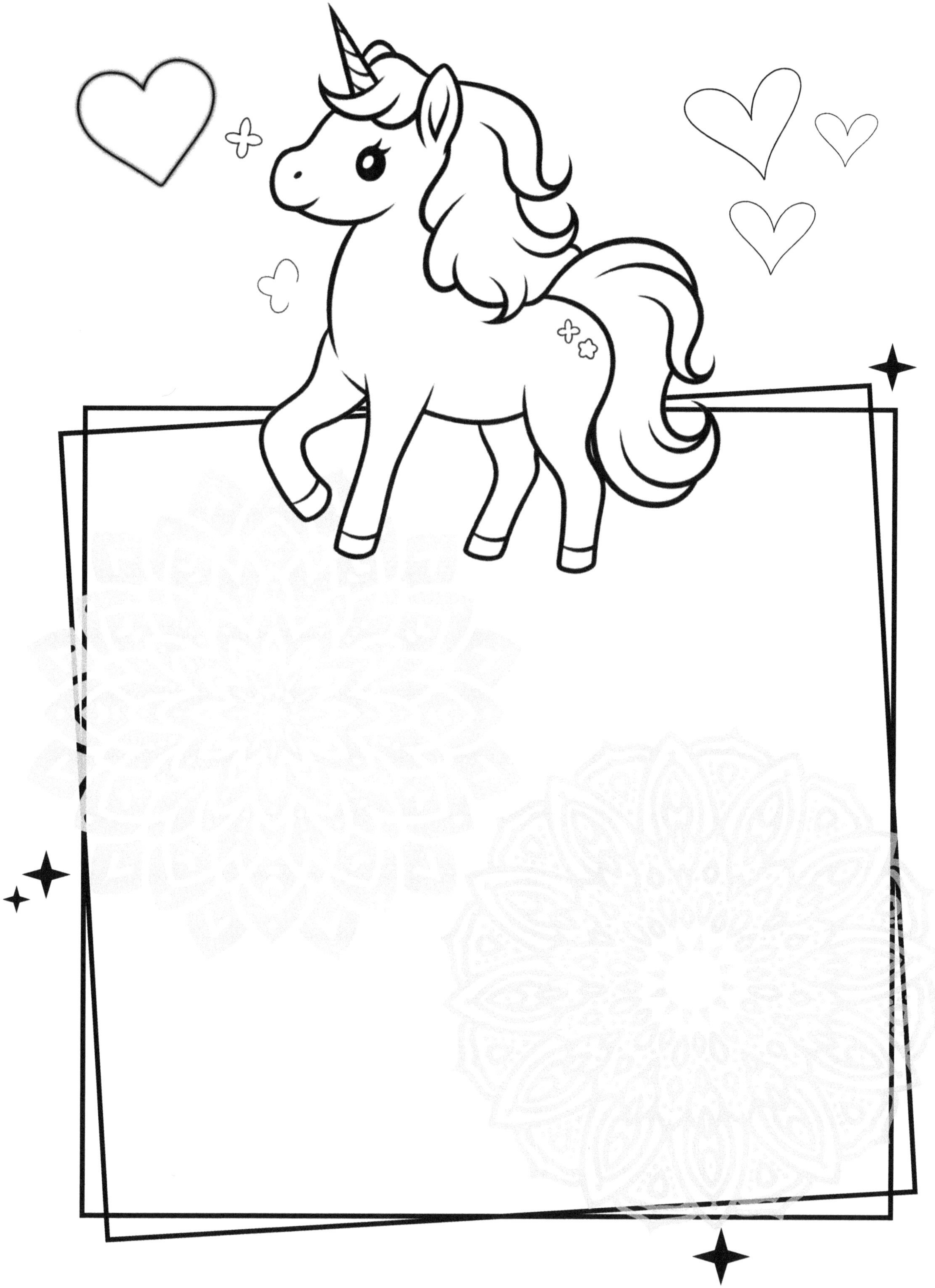

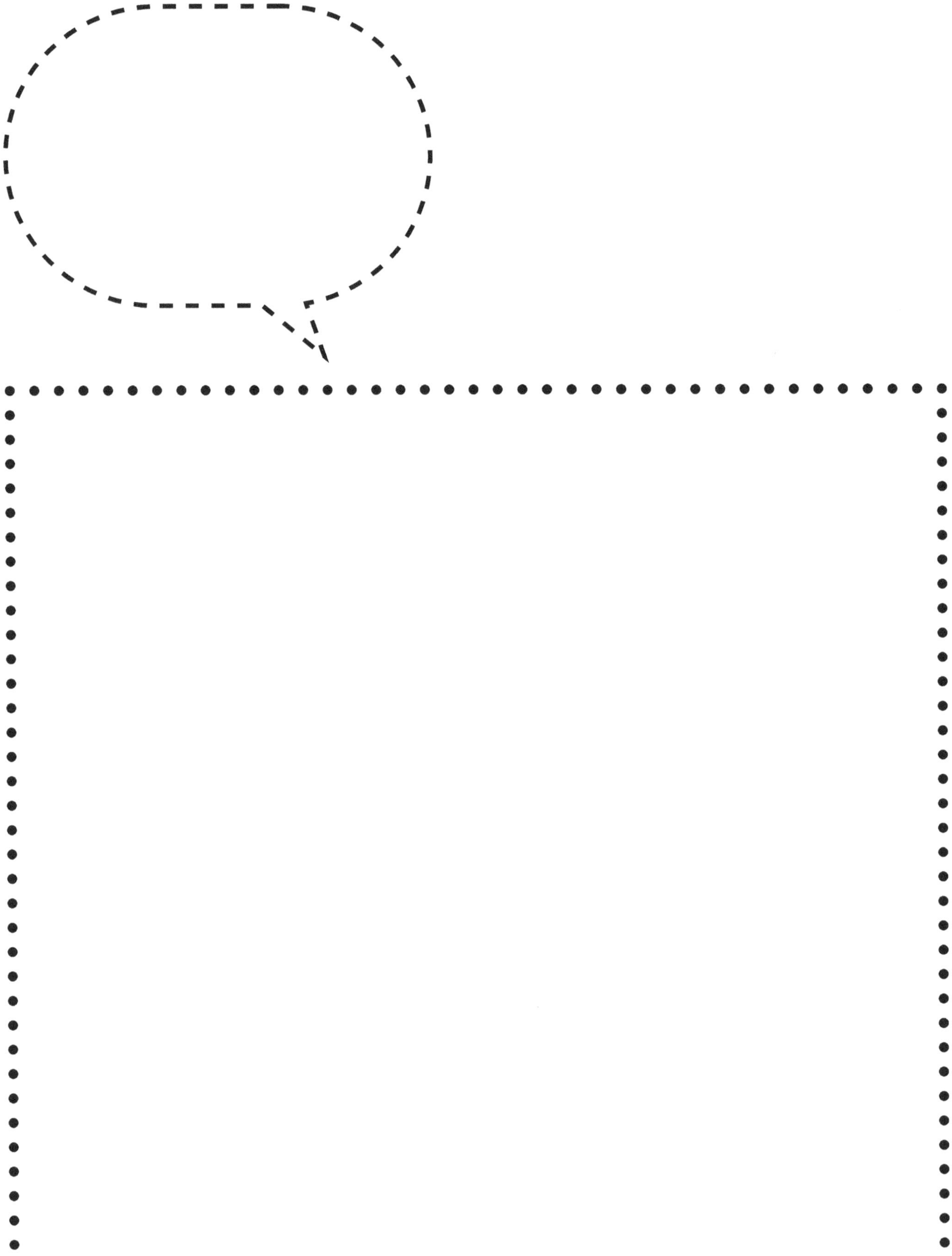

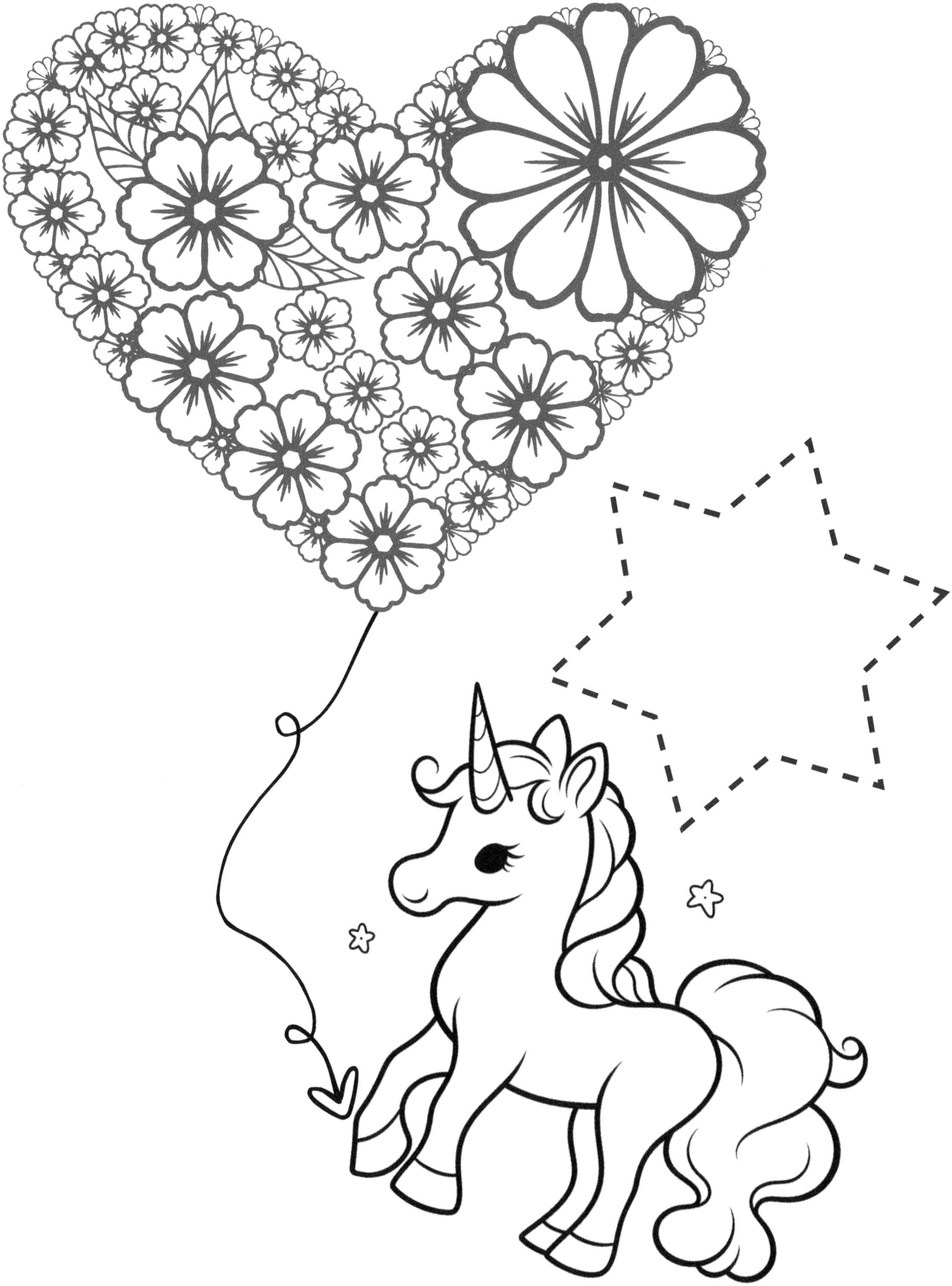

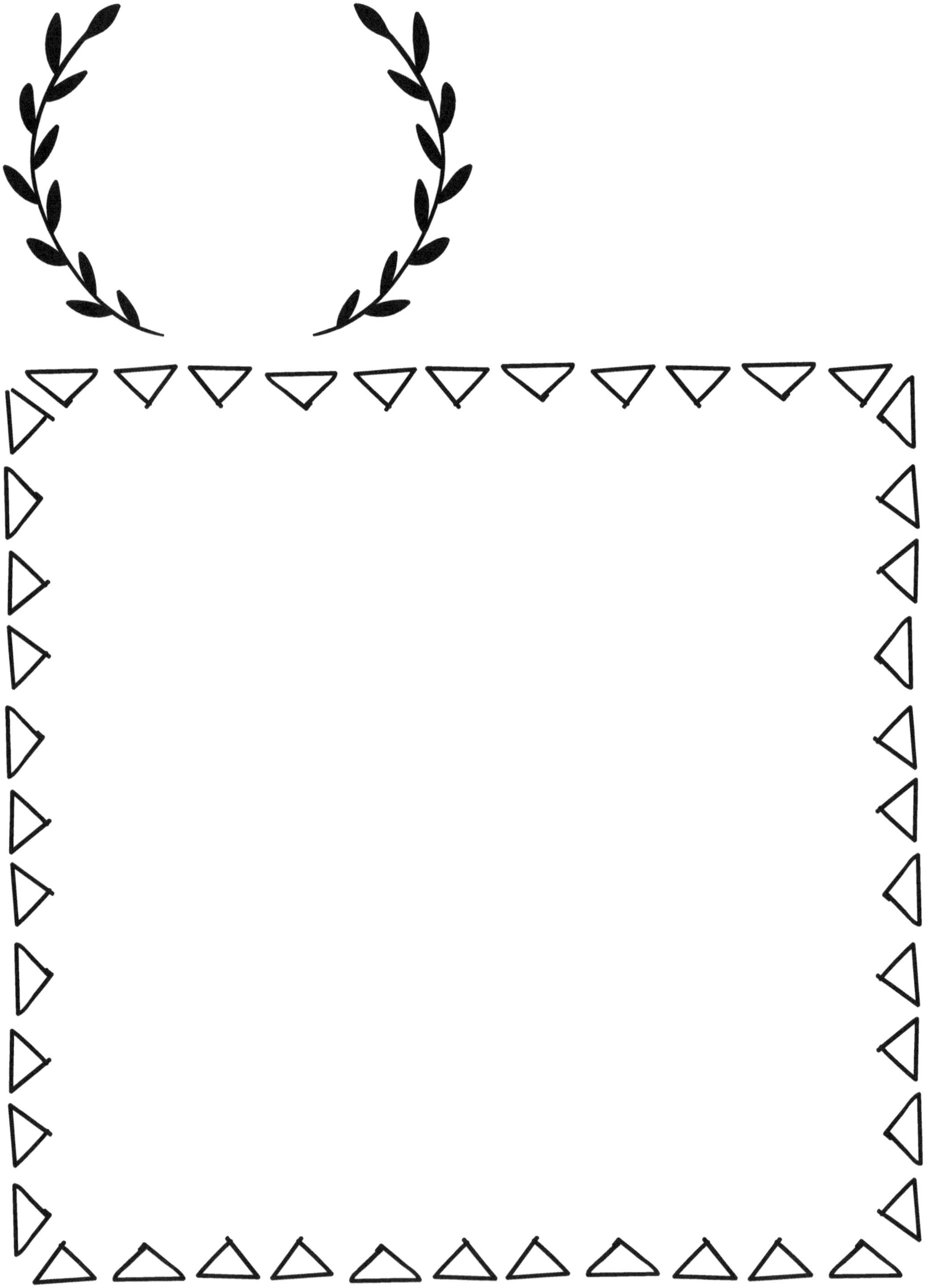

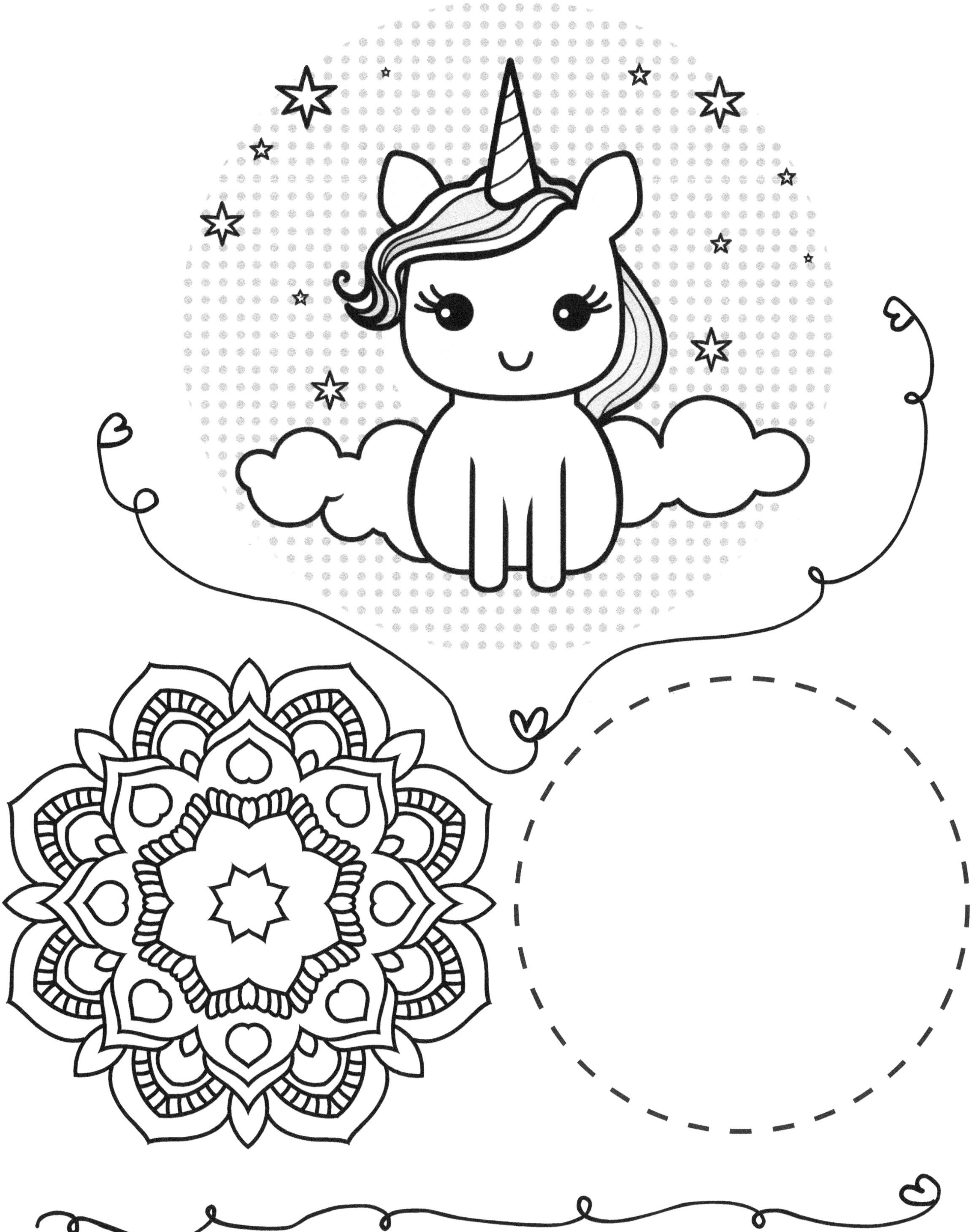

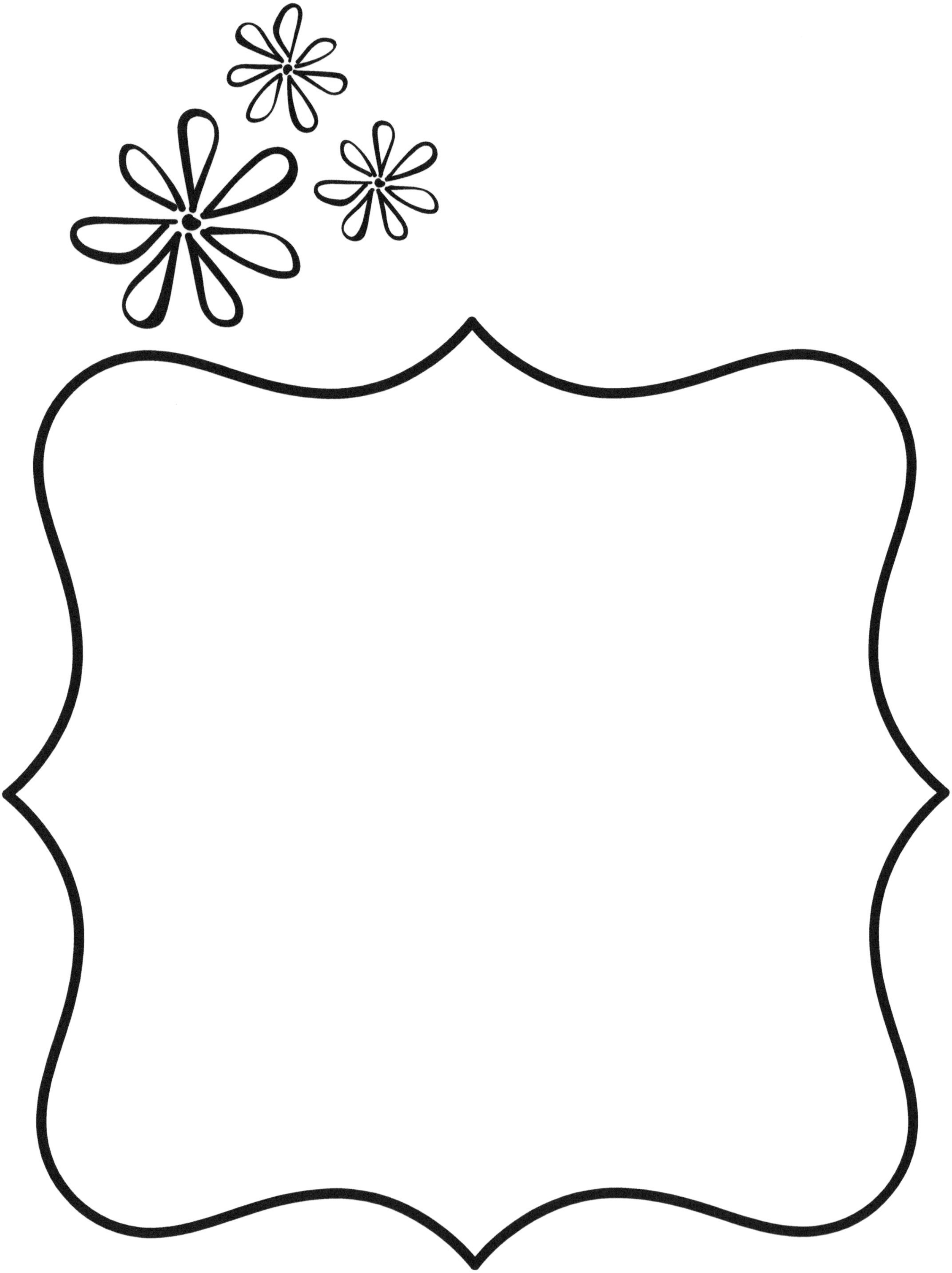

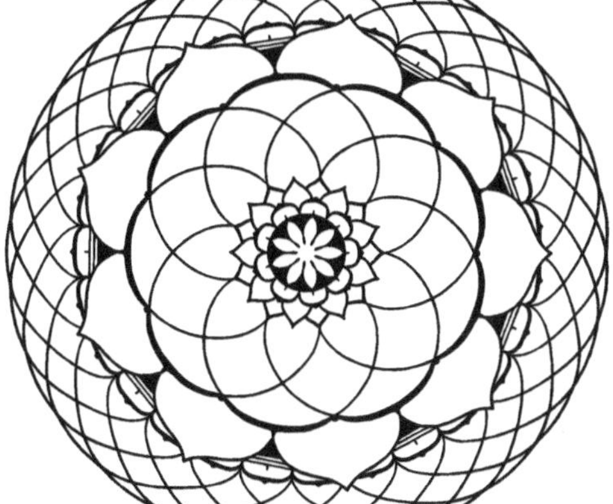
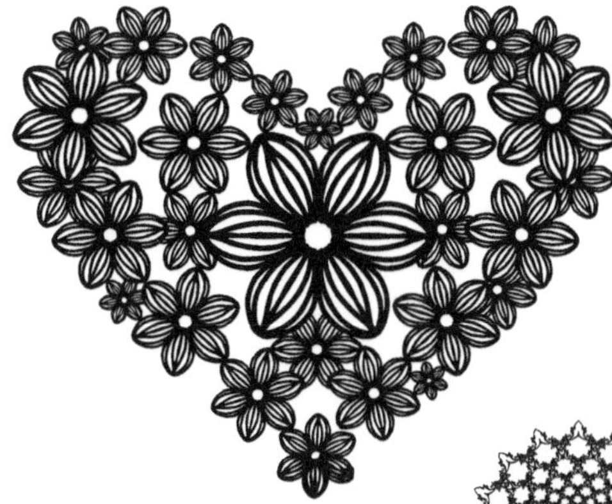
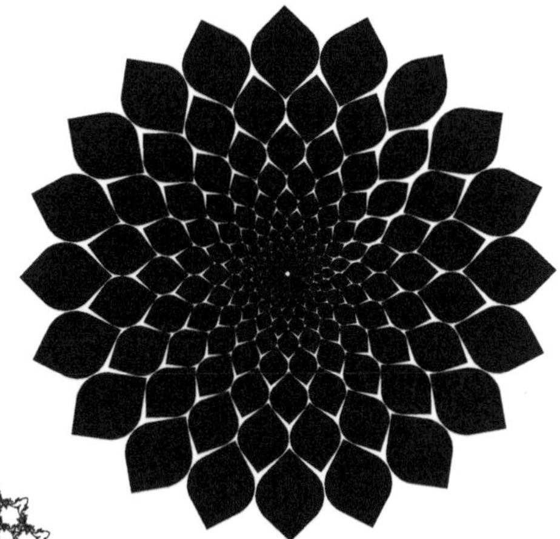
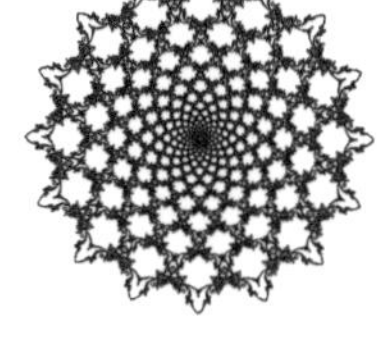
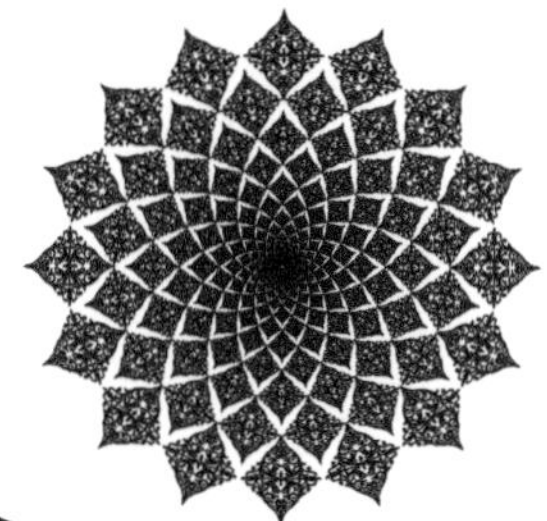

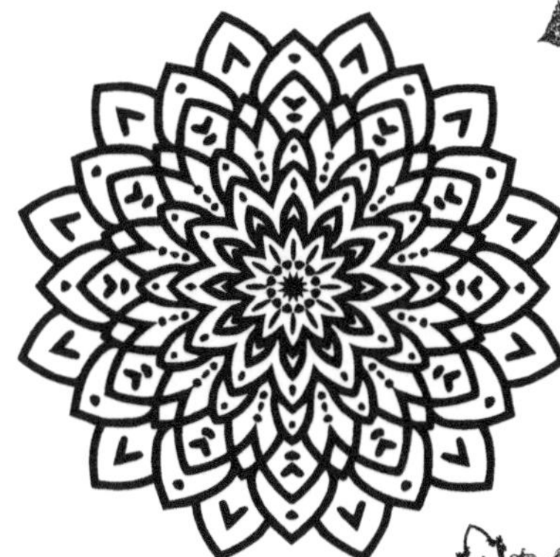

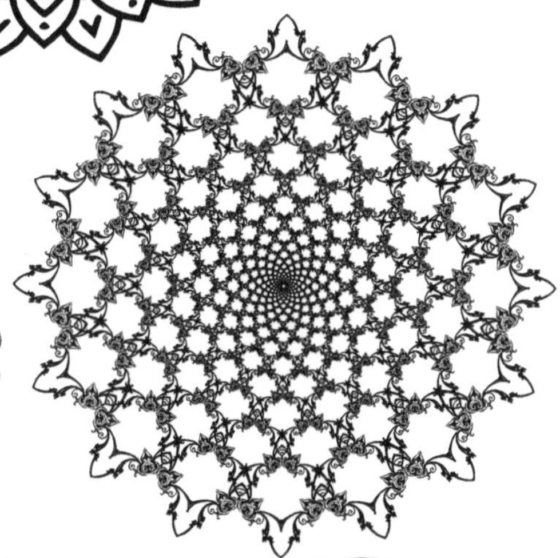

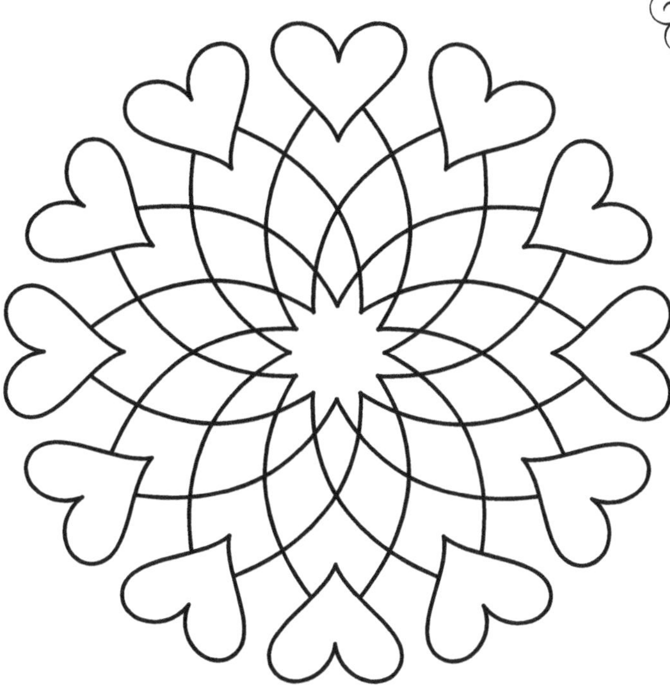

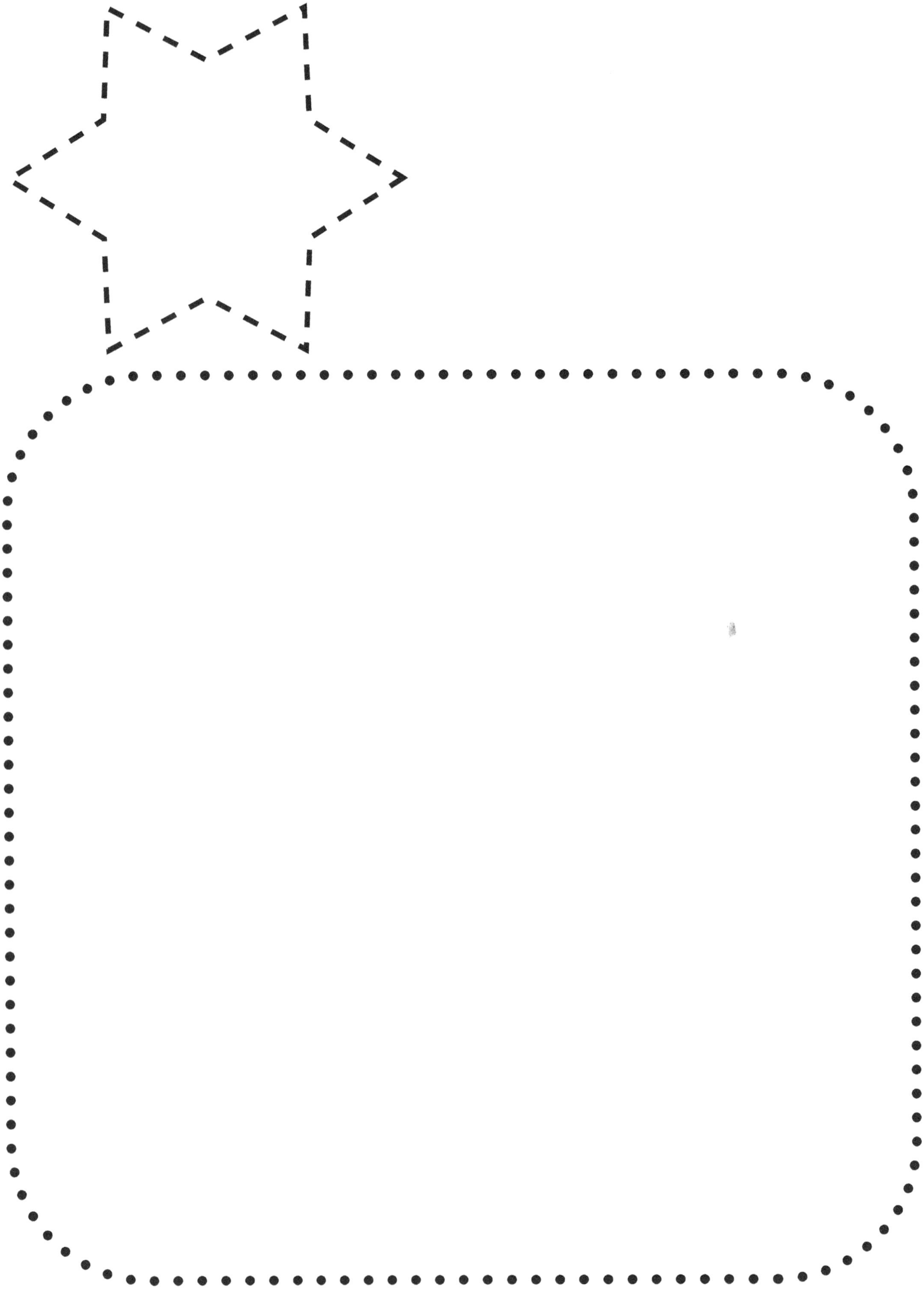

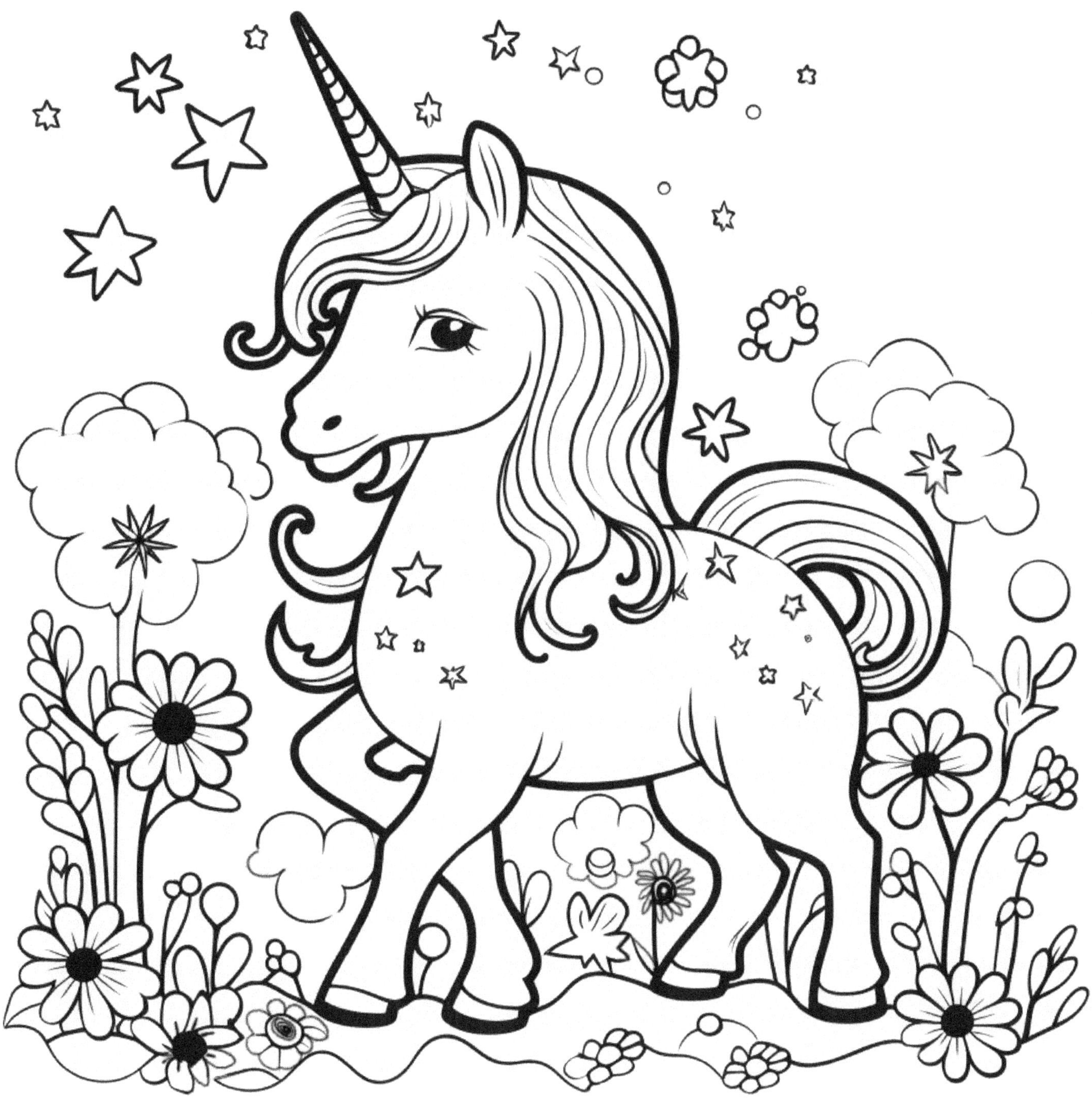

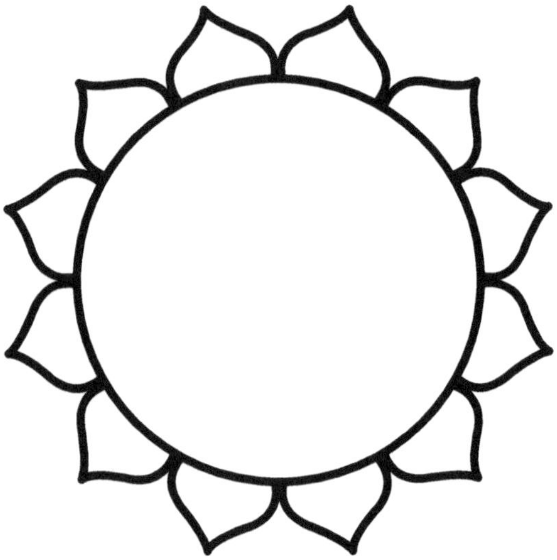

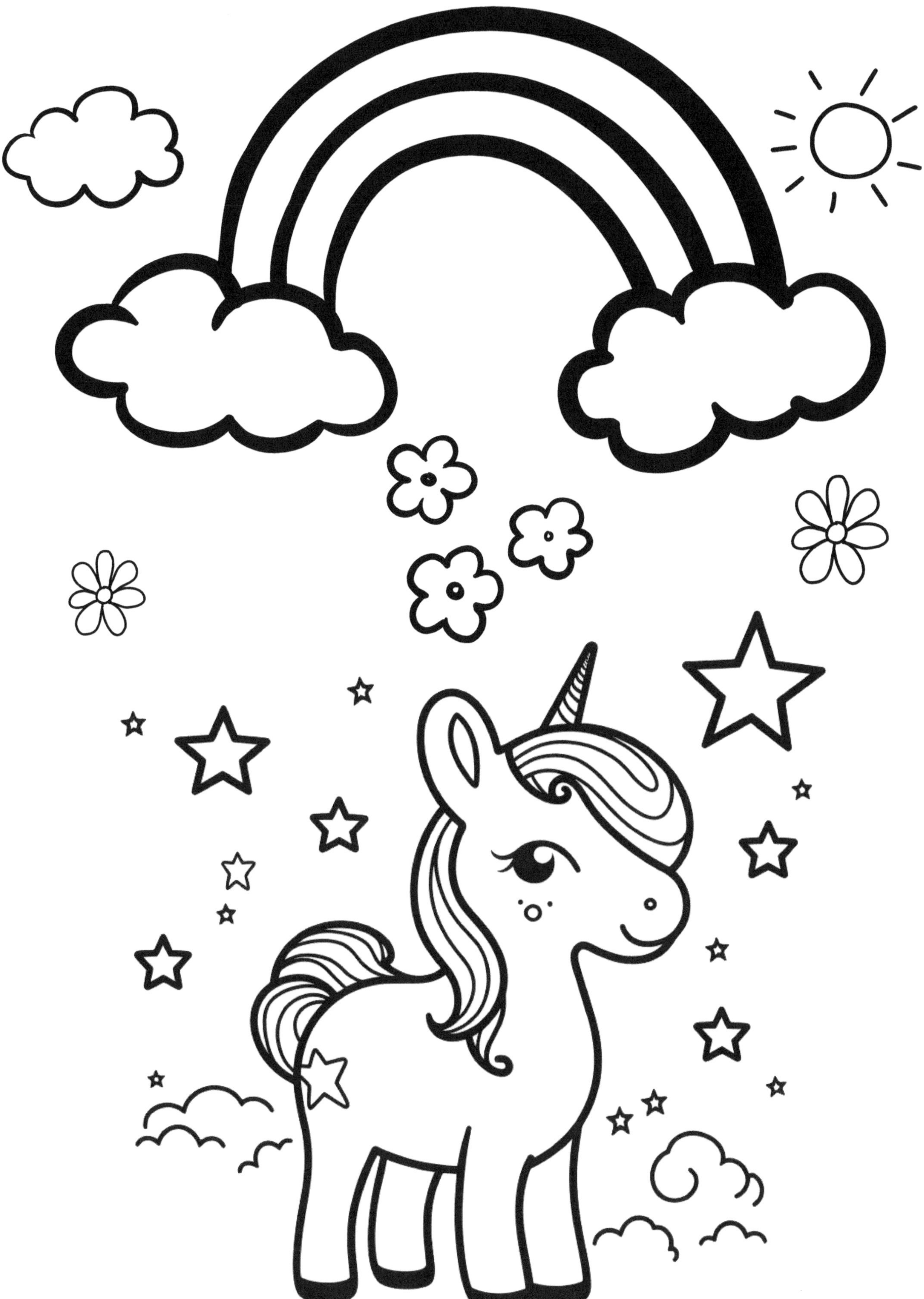

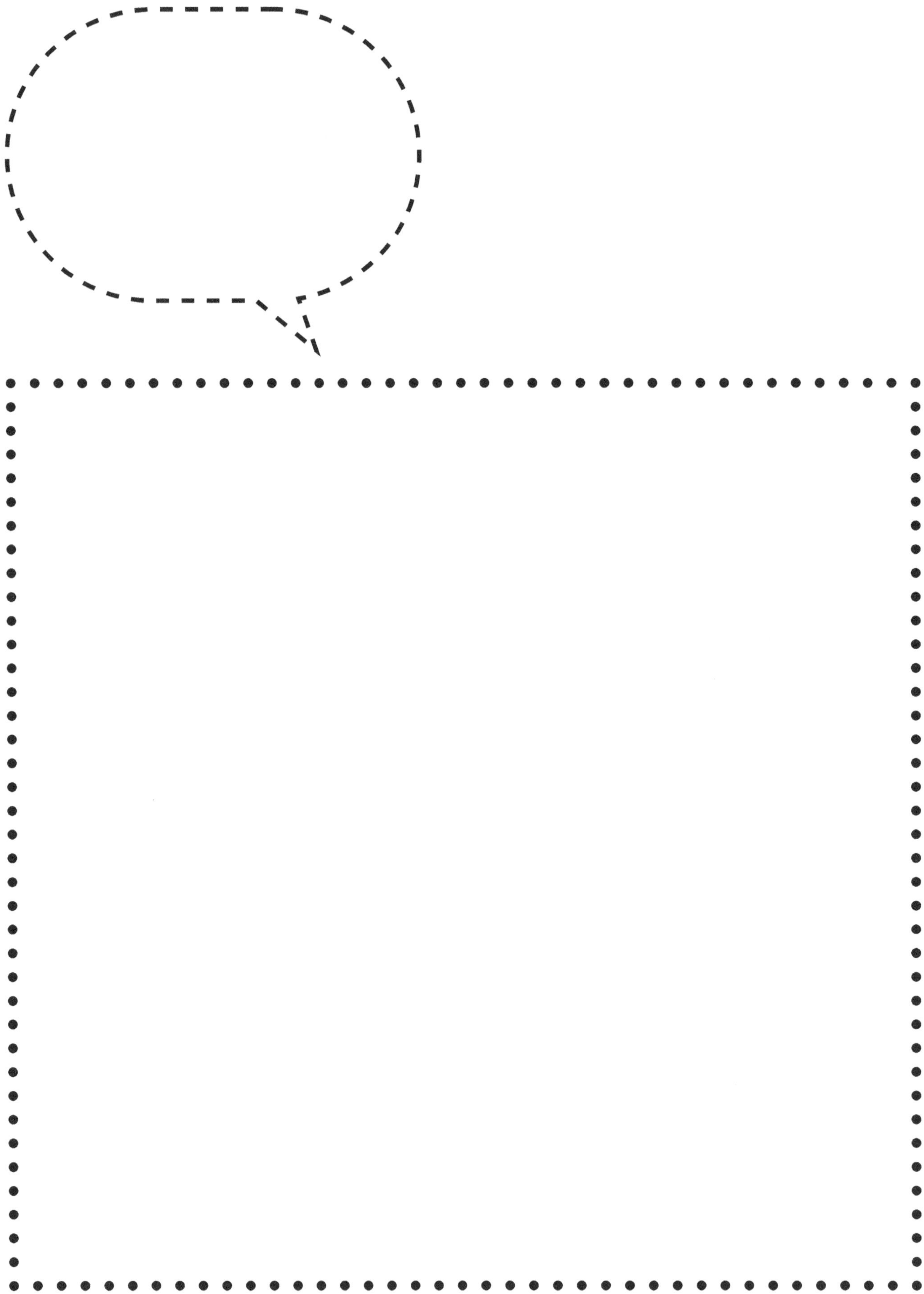

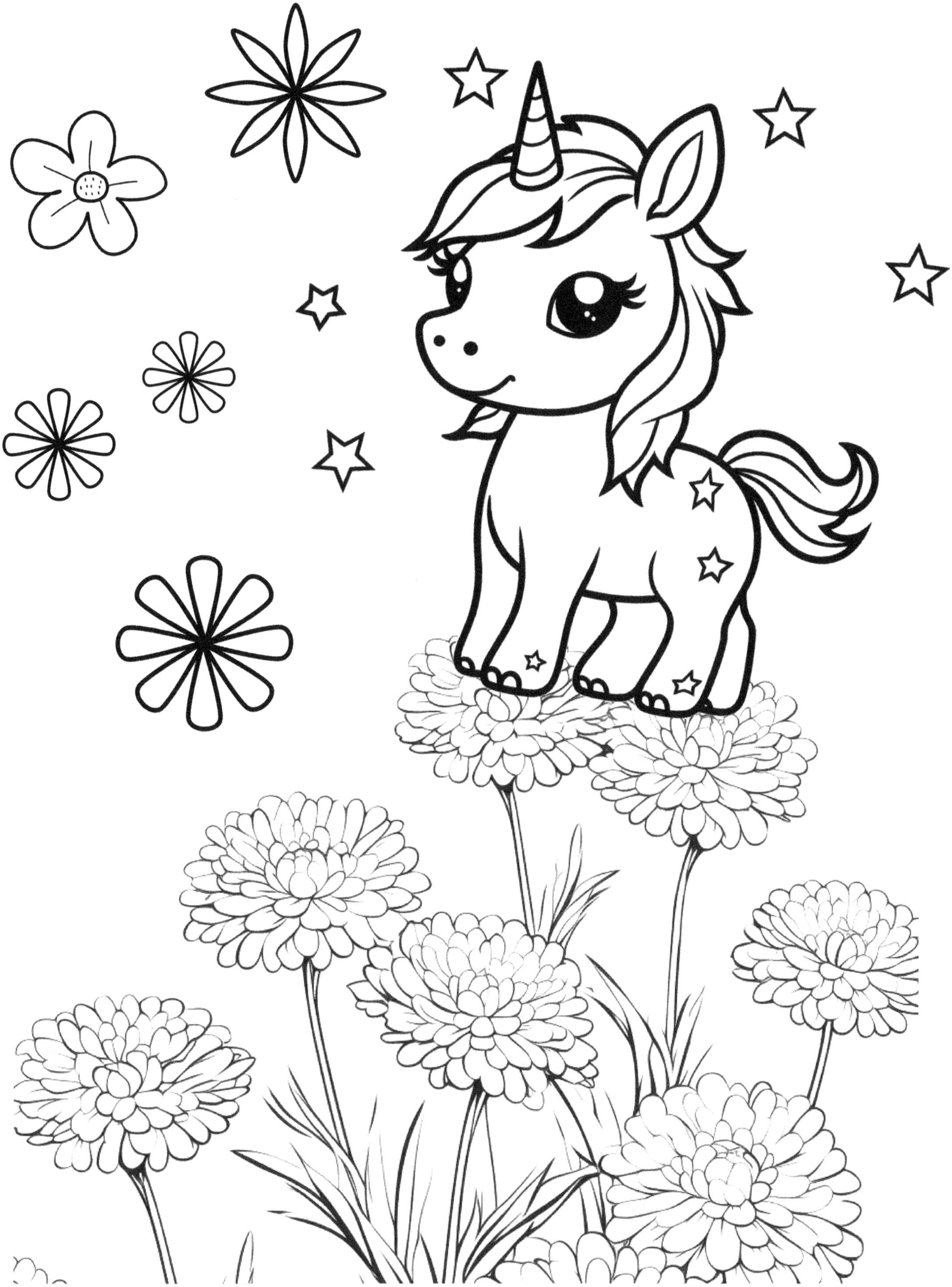

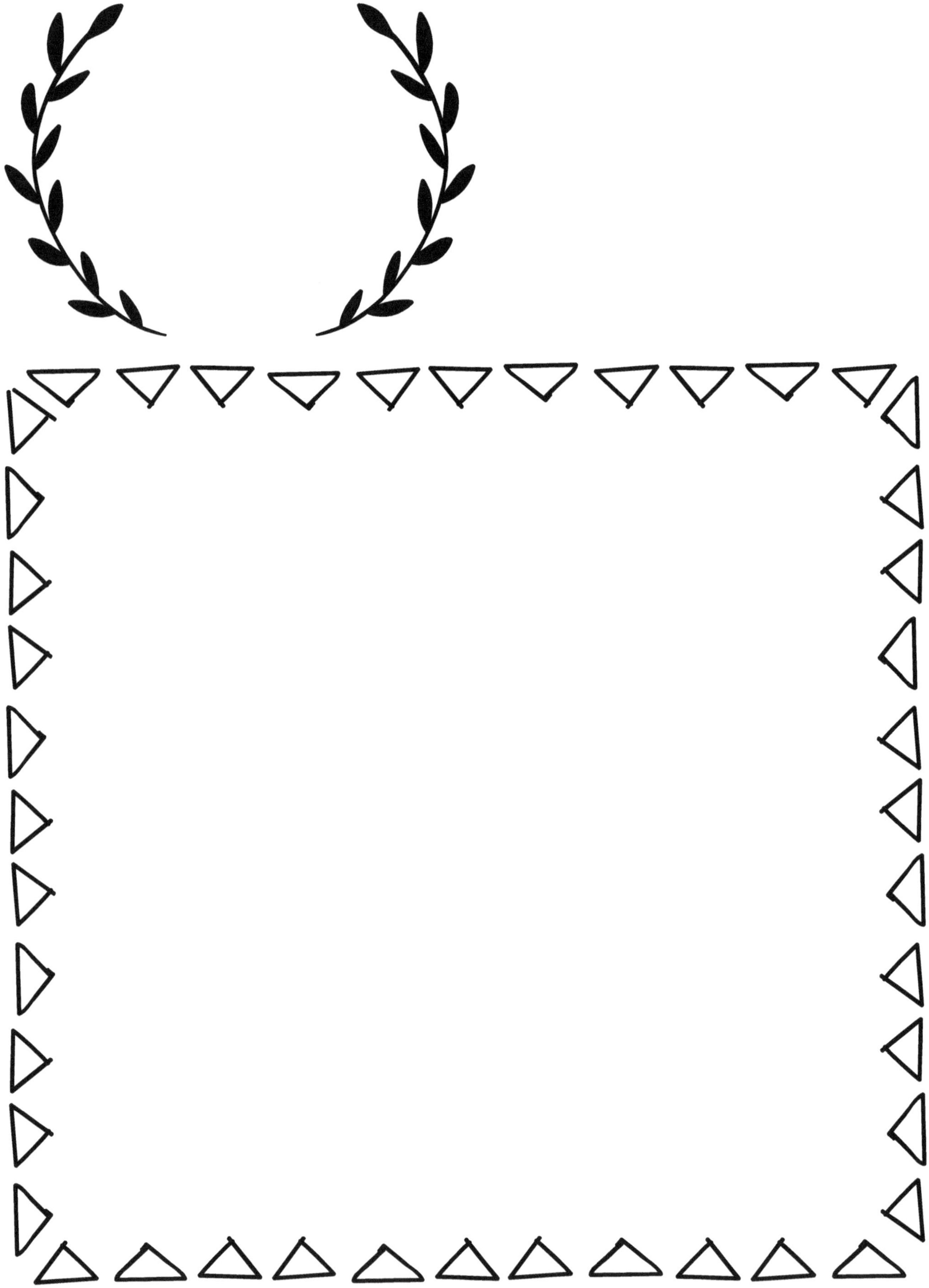

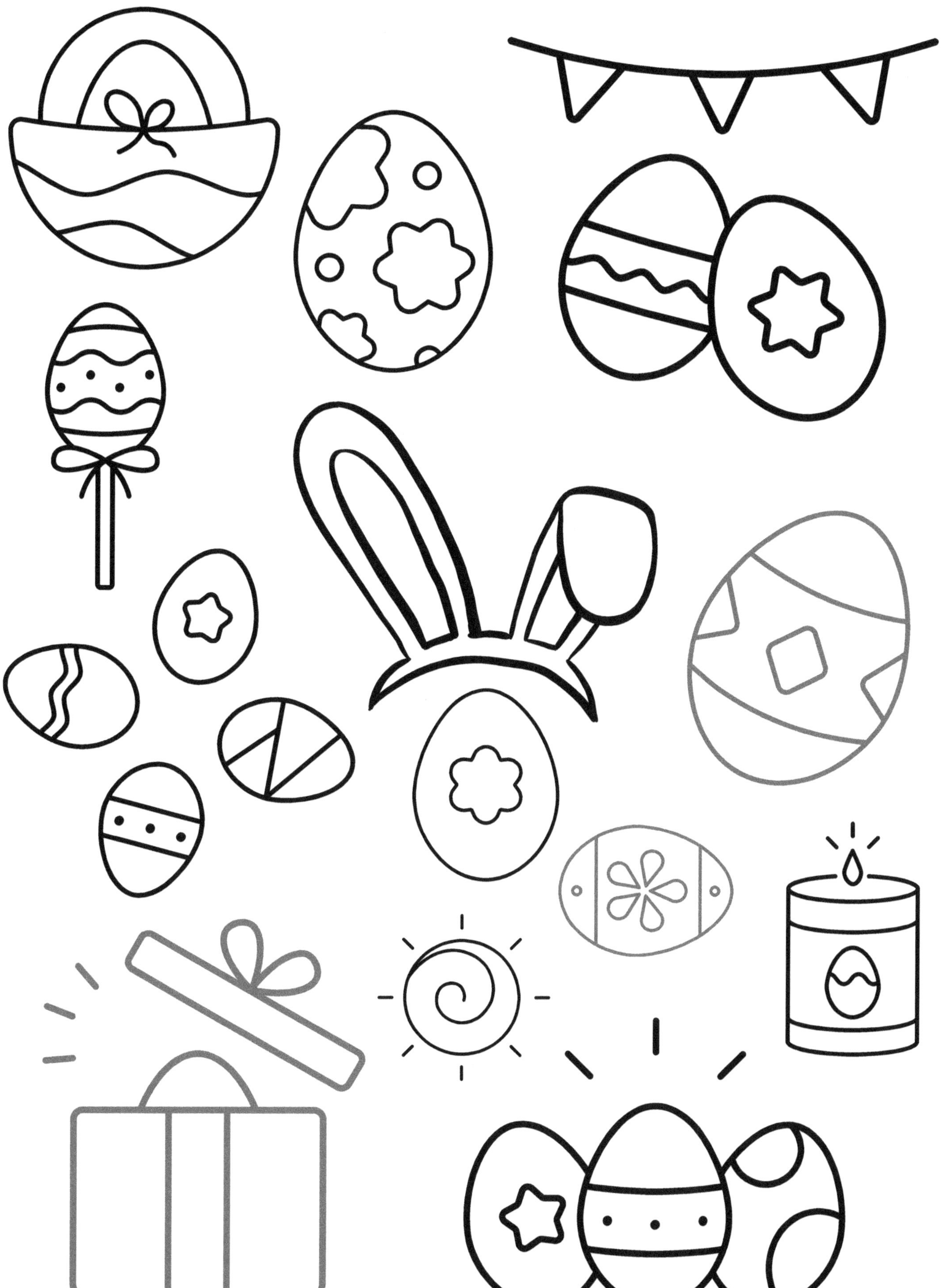

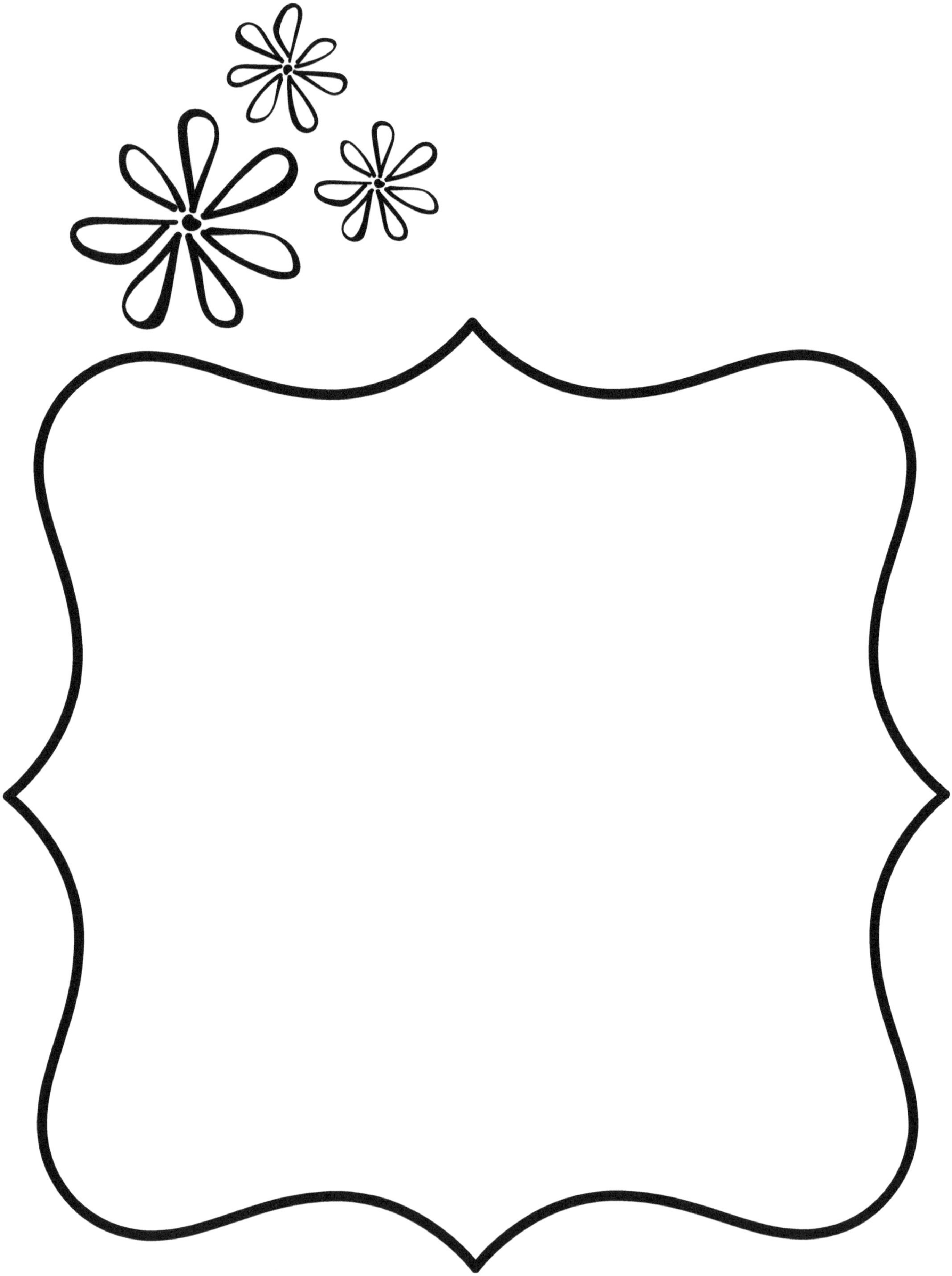

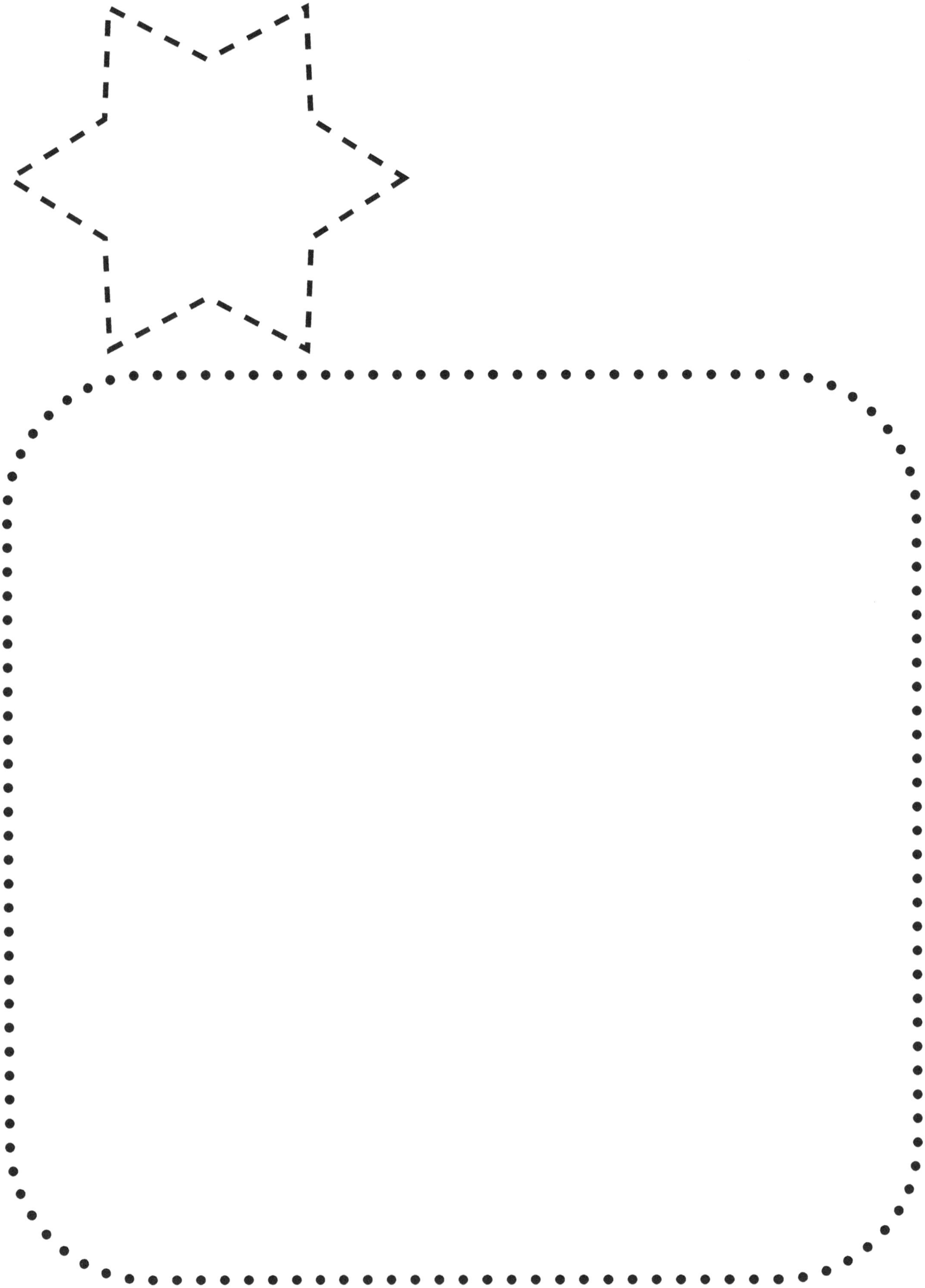

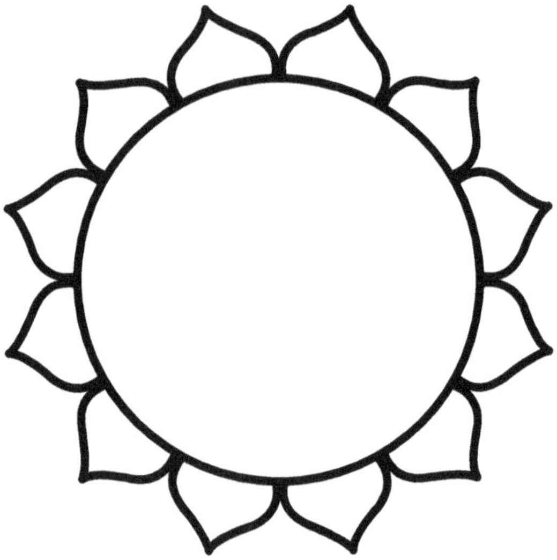

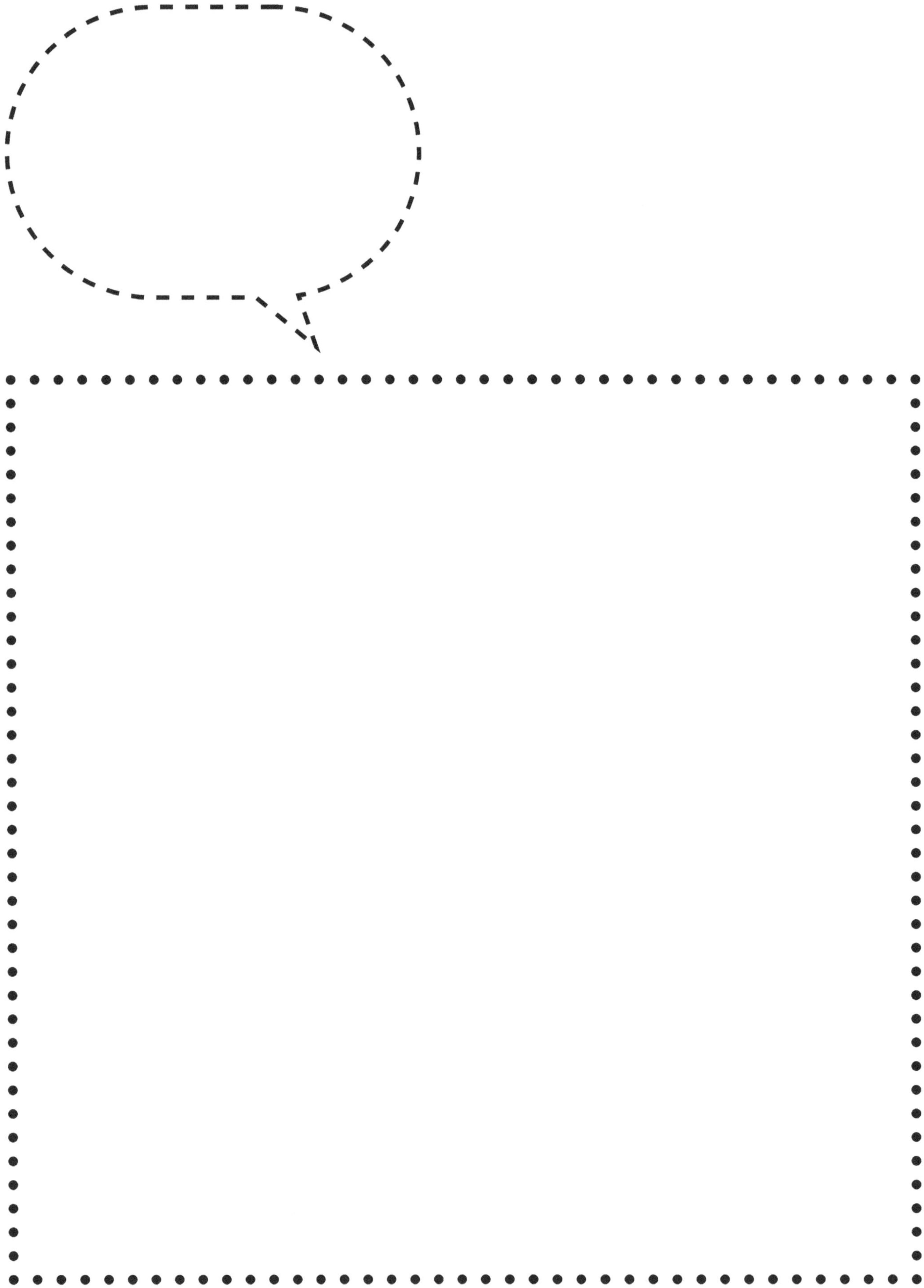

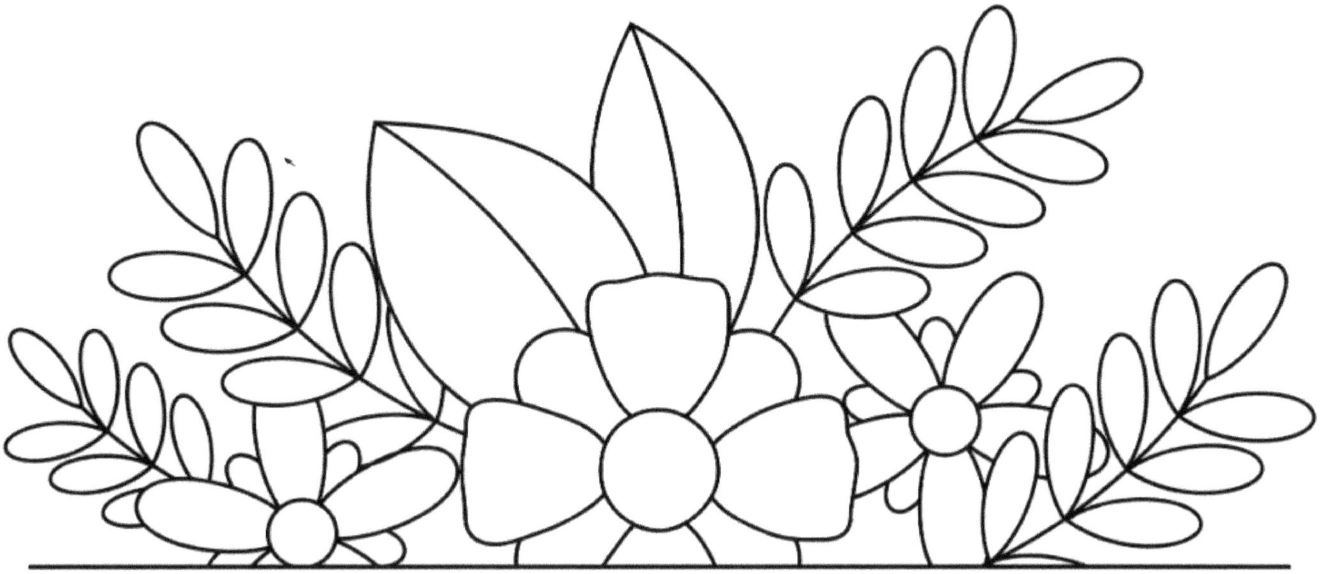

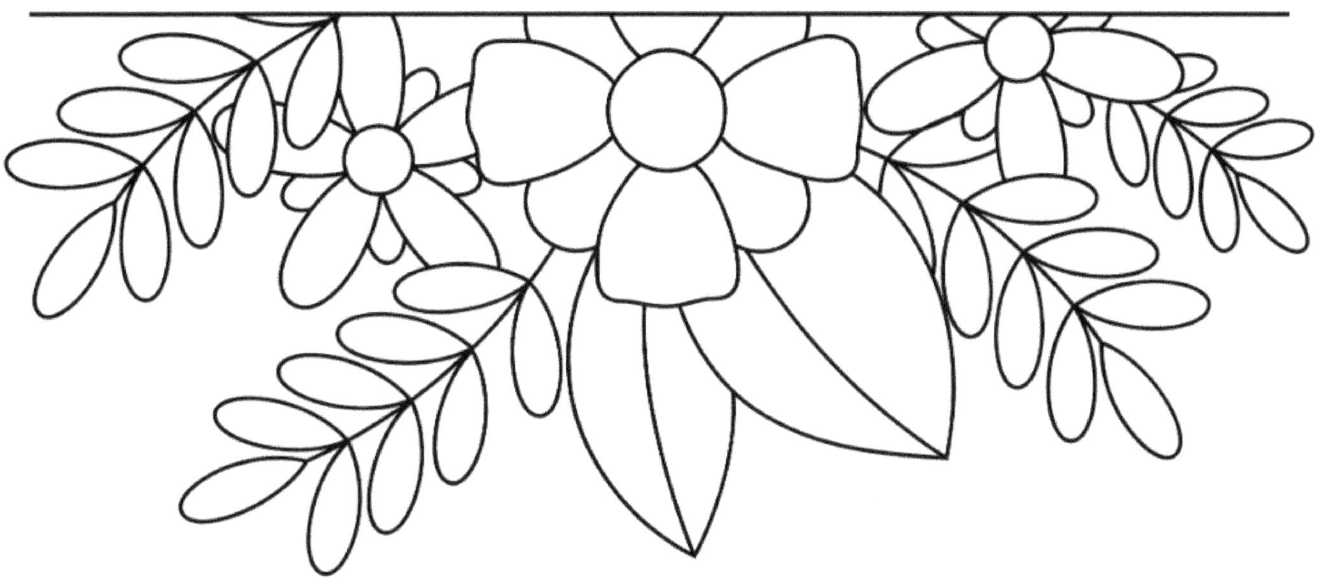

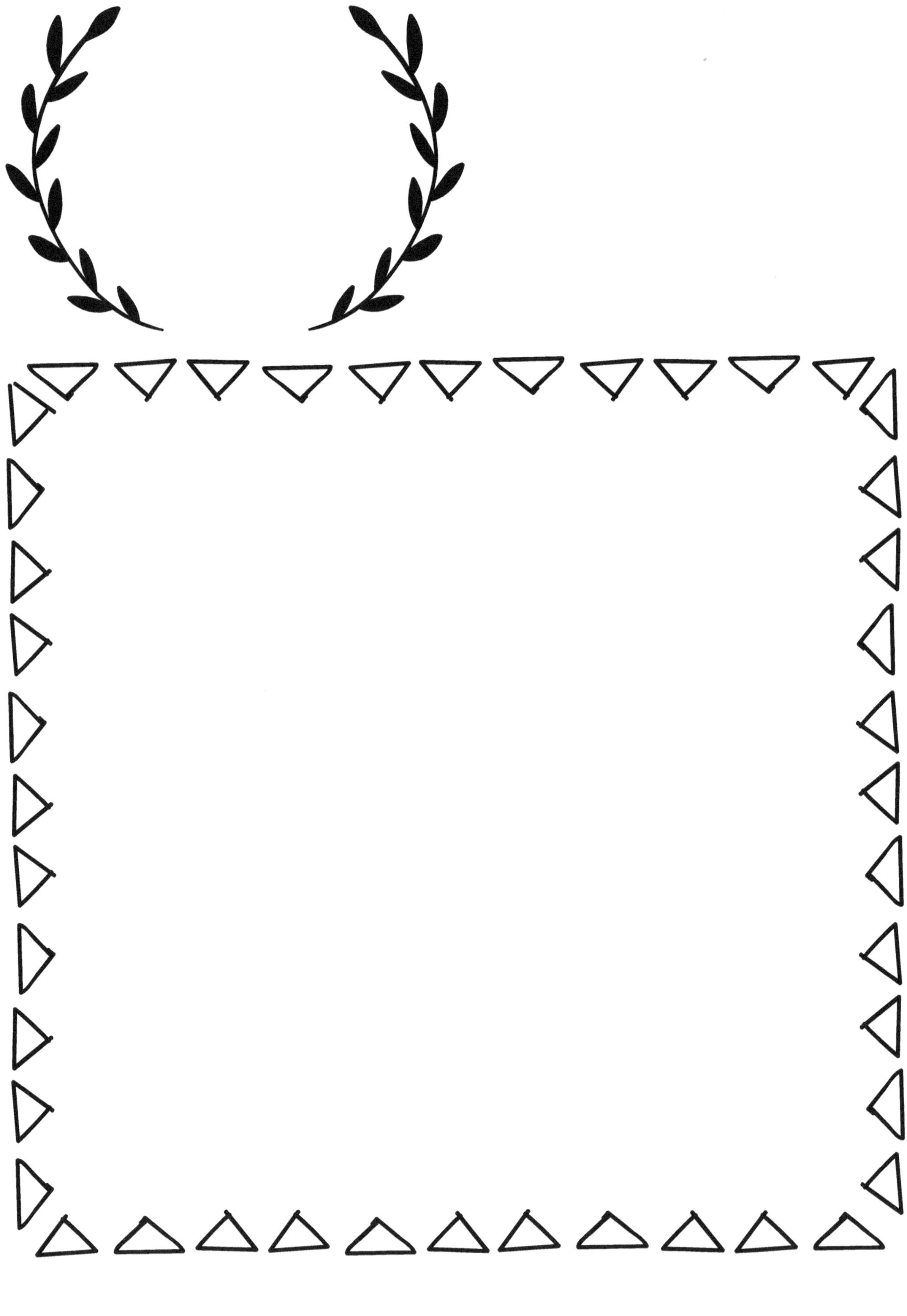

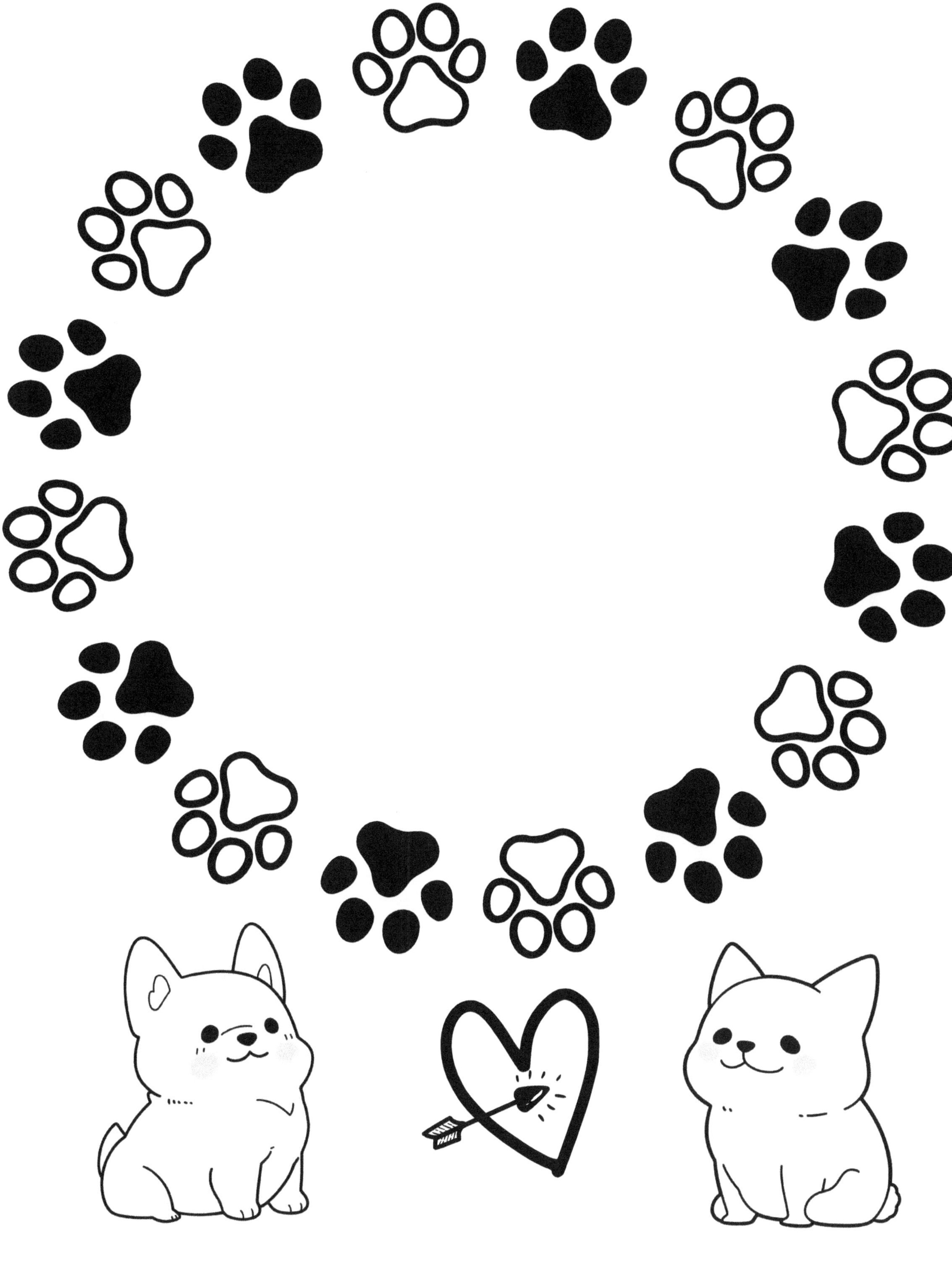

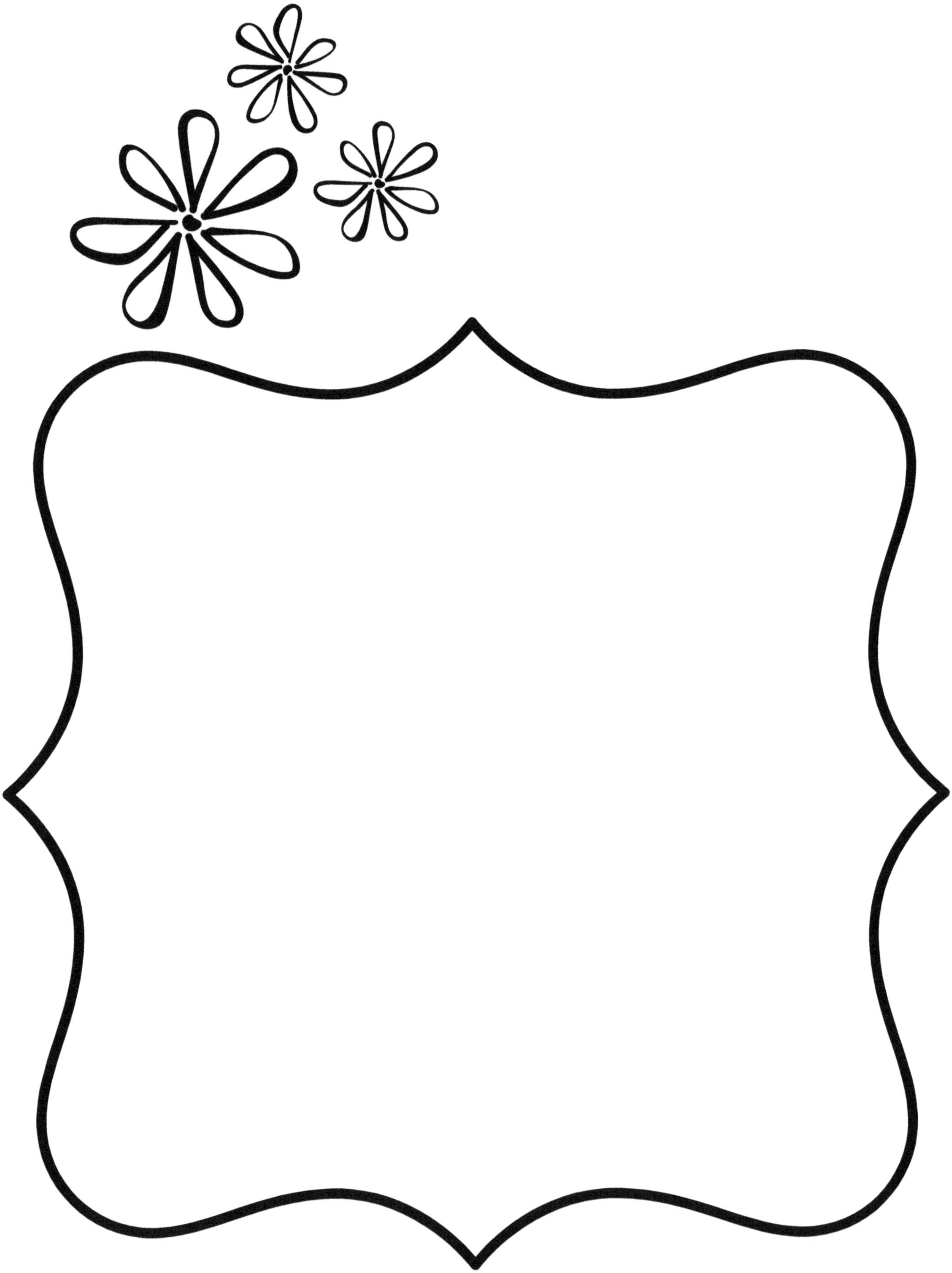

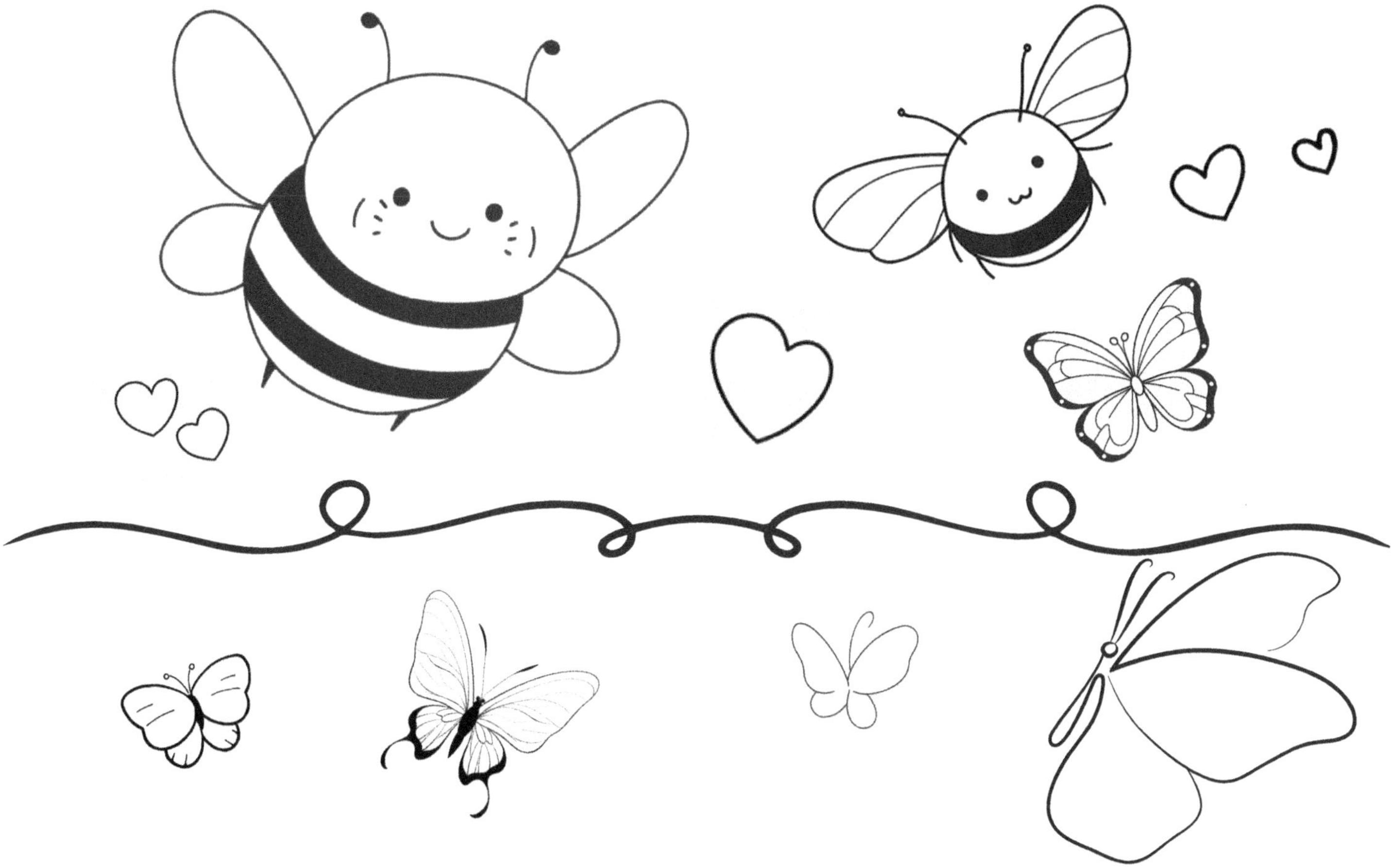

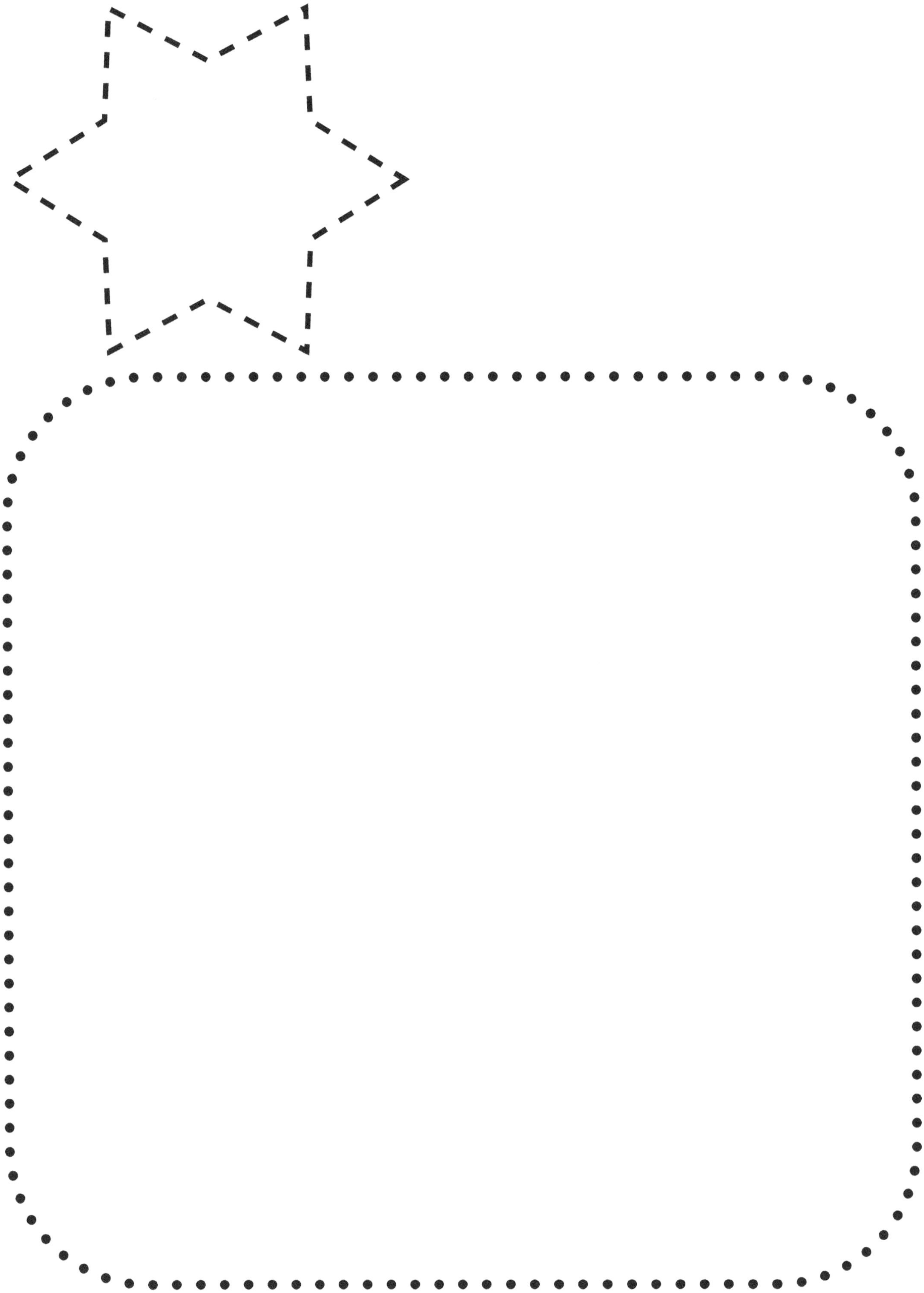

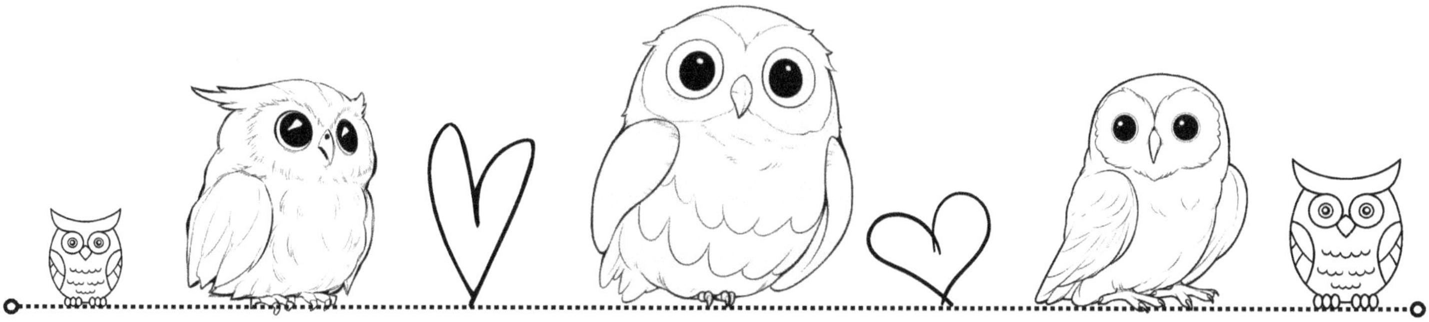

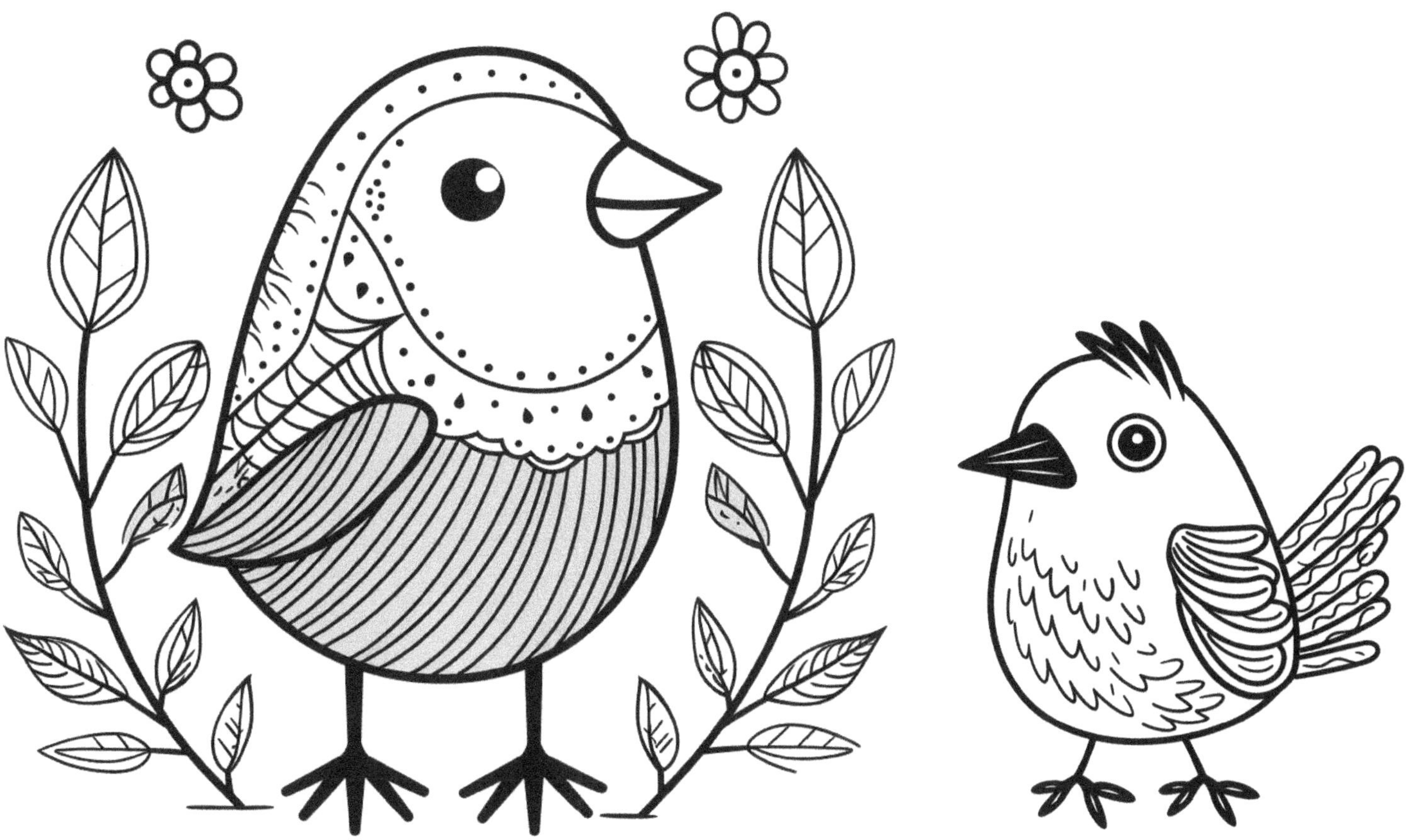

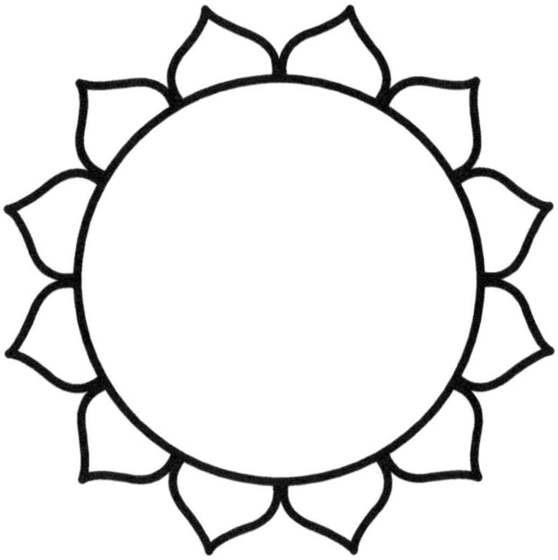

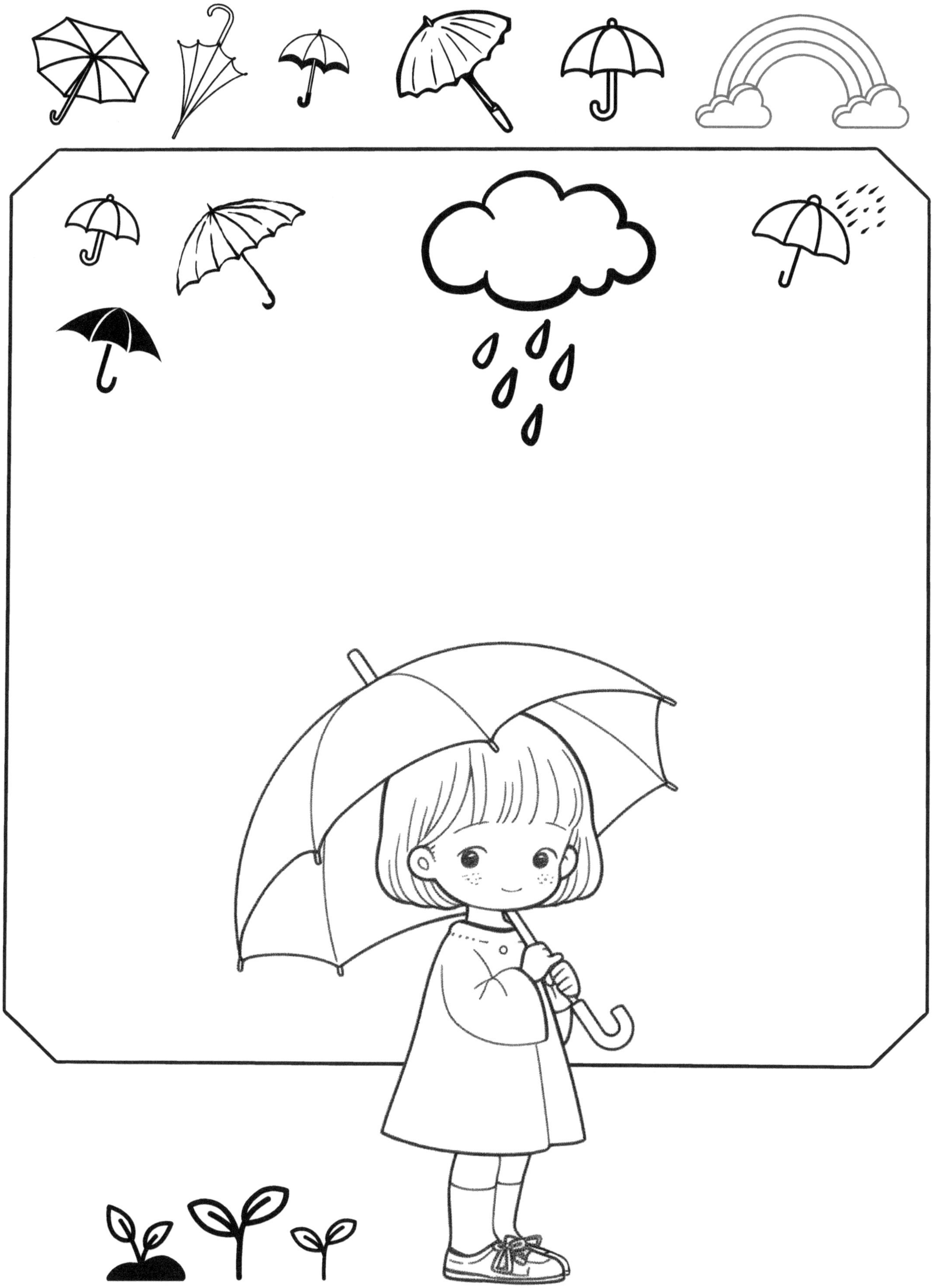

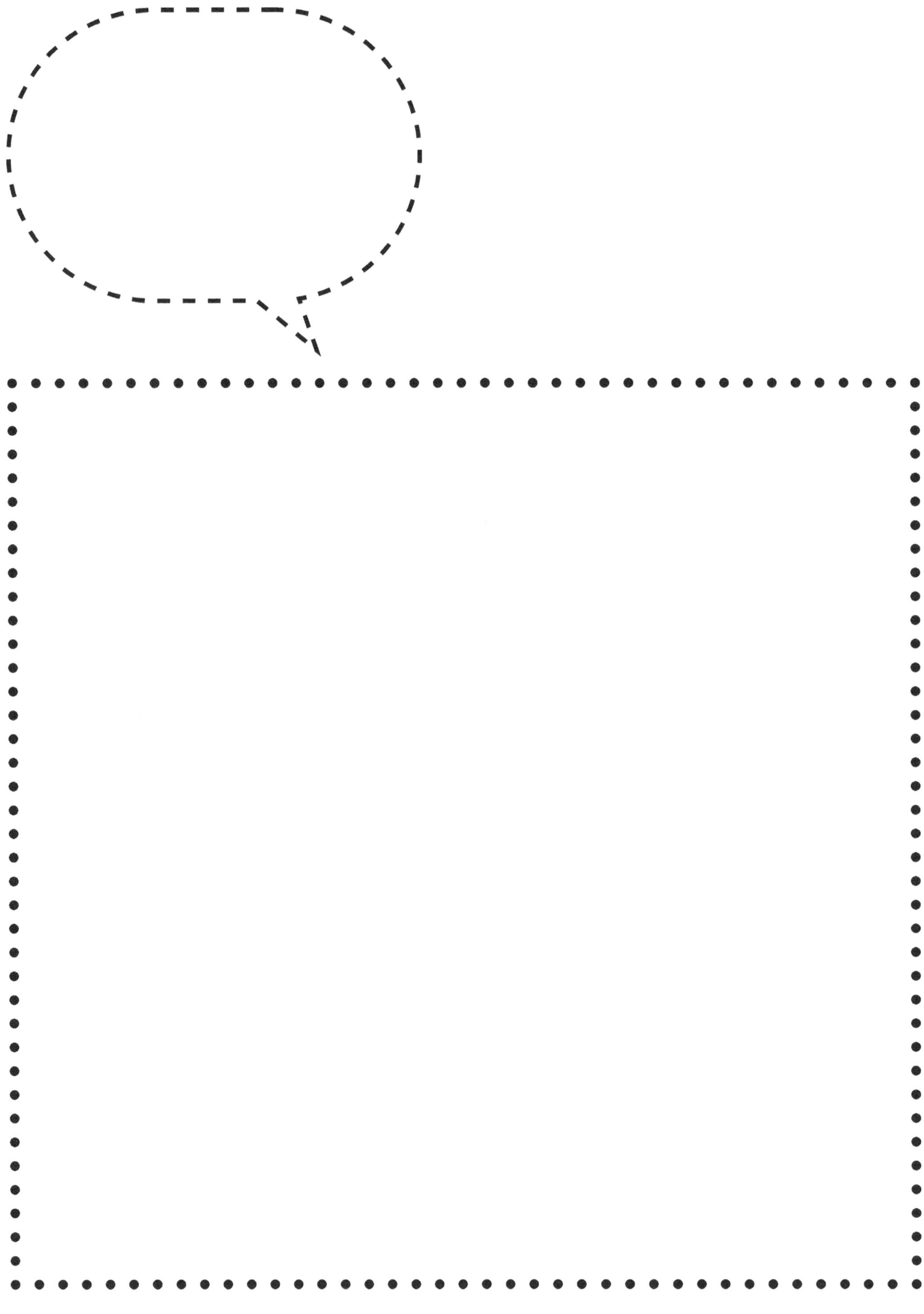

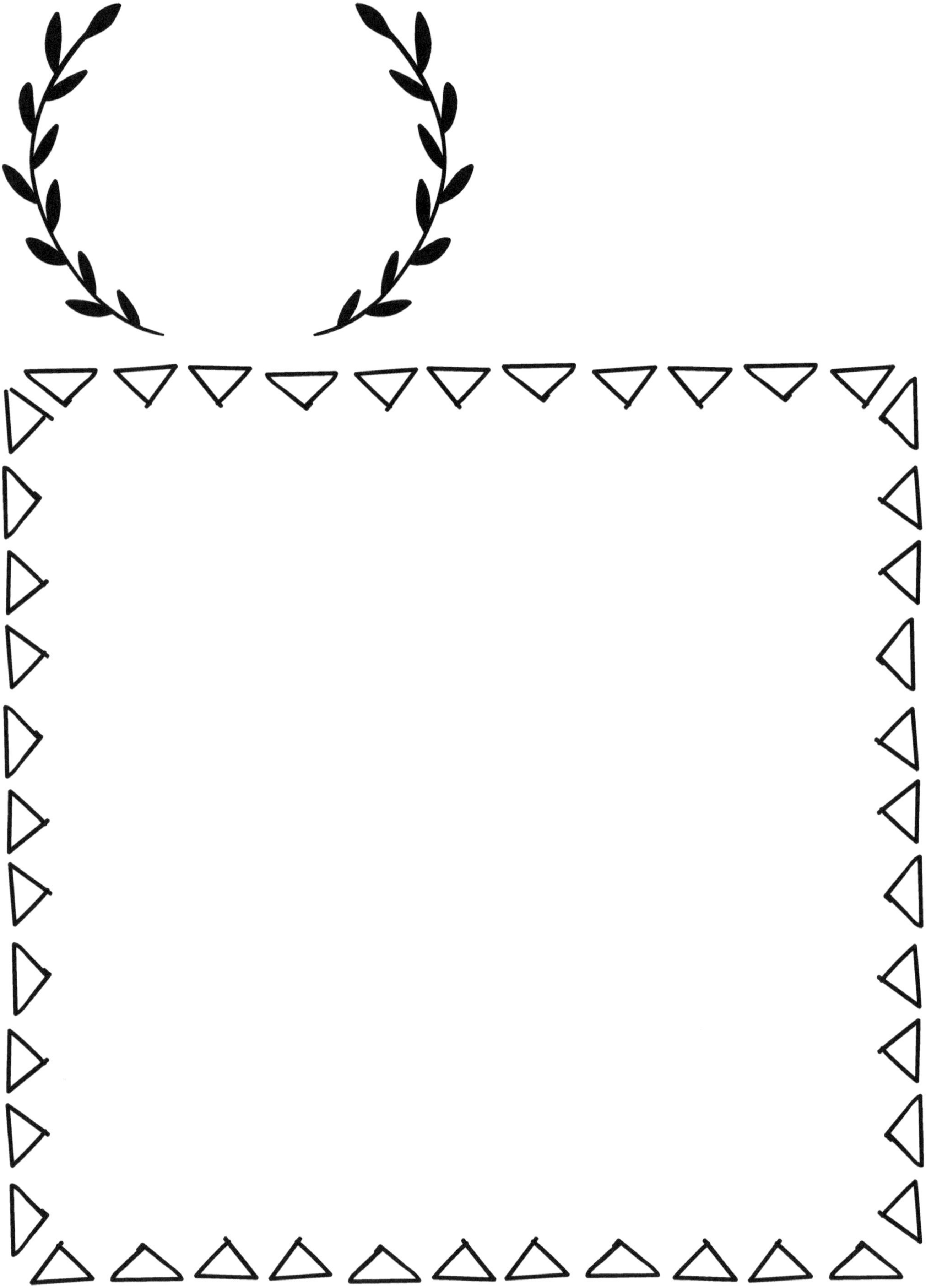

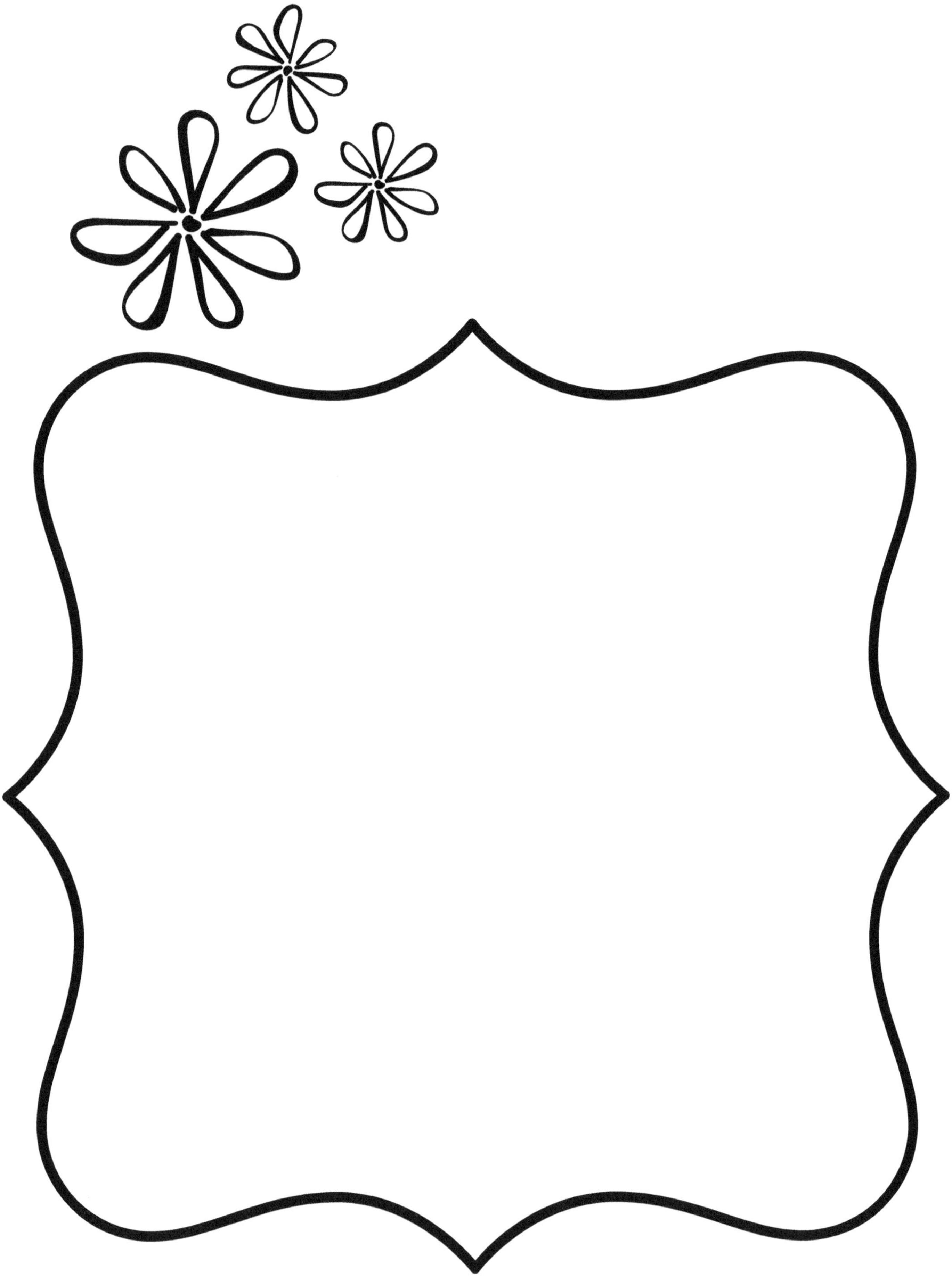

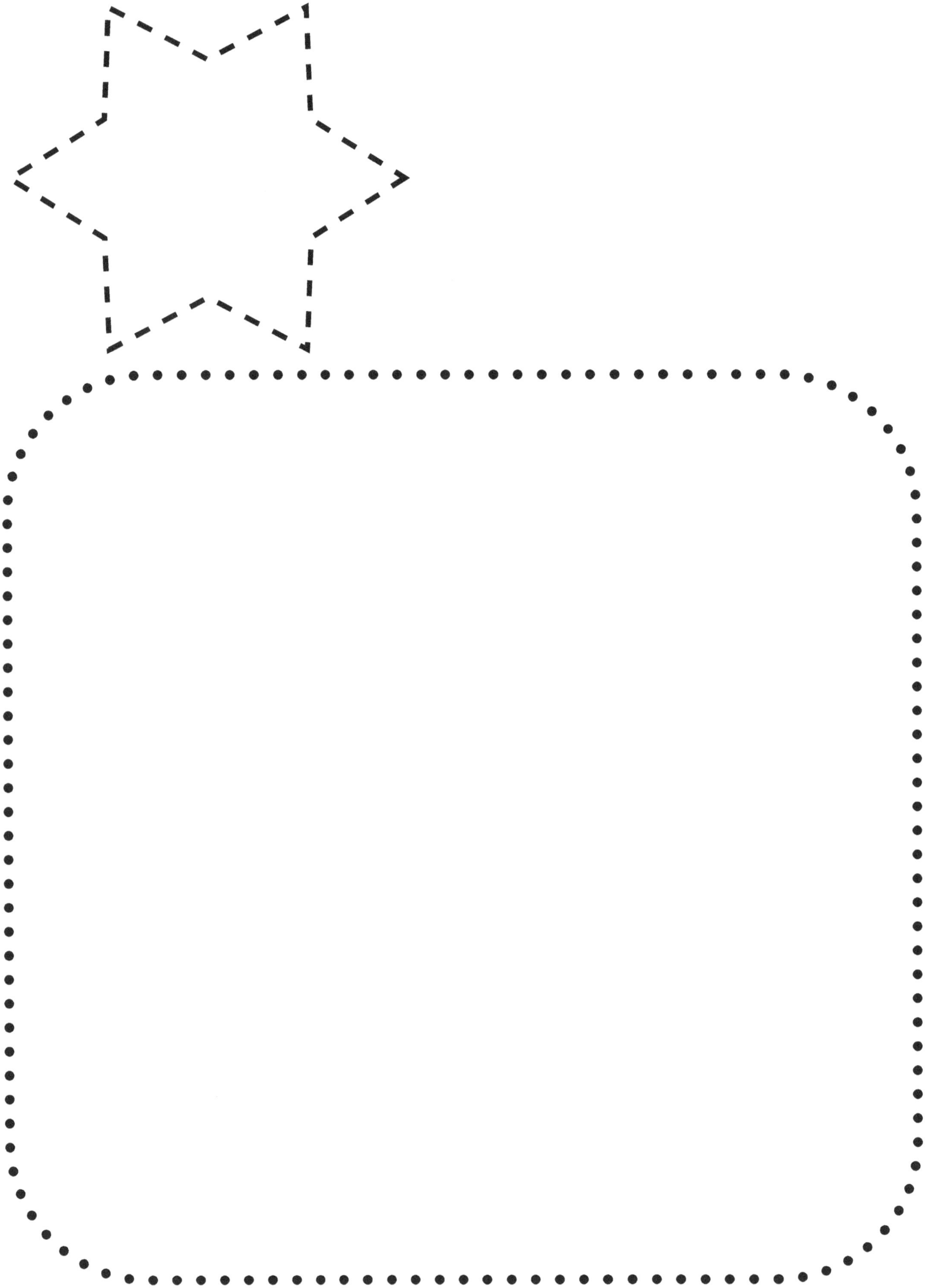

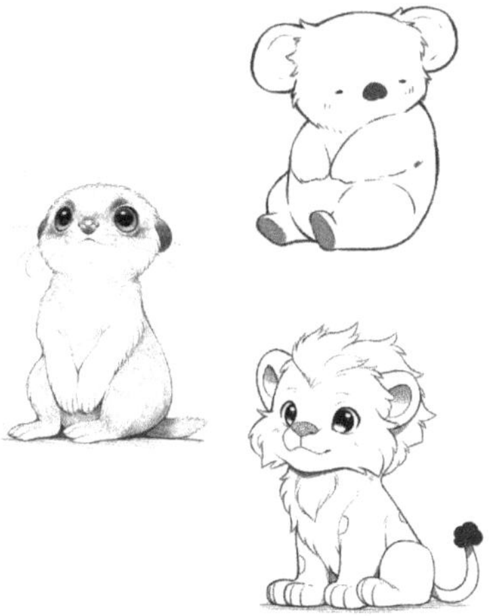

ZOO

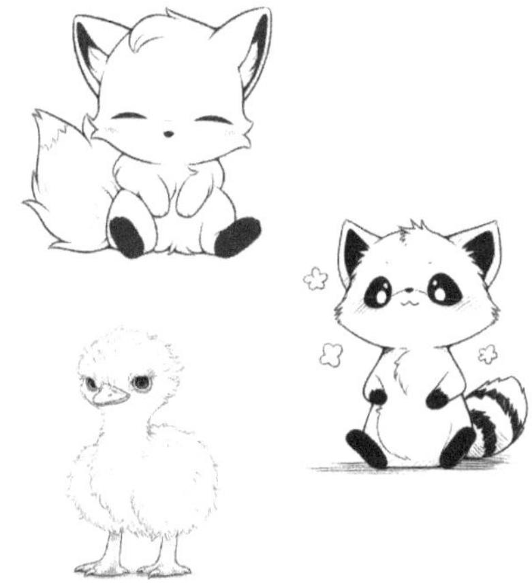

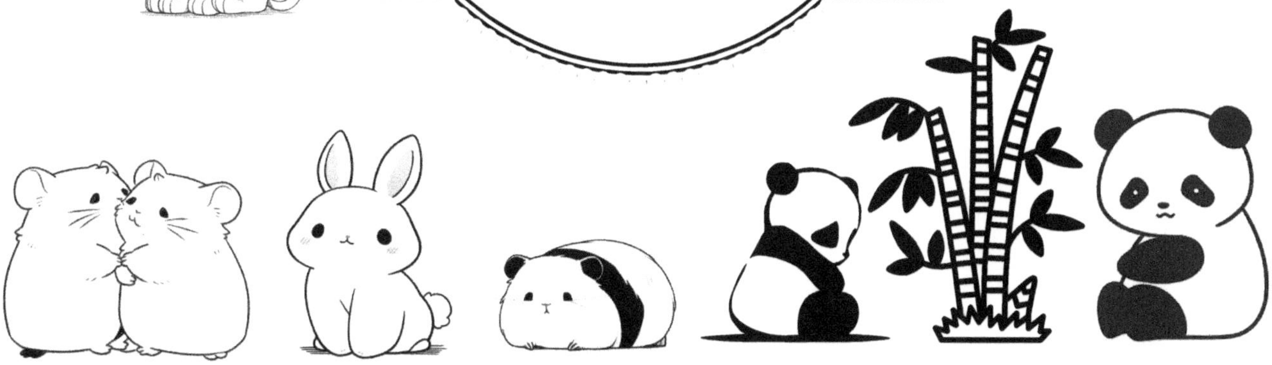

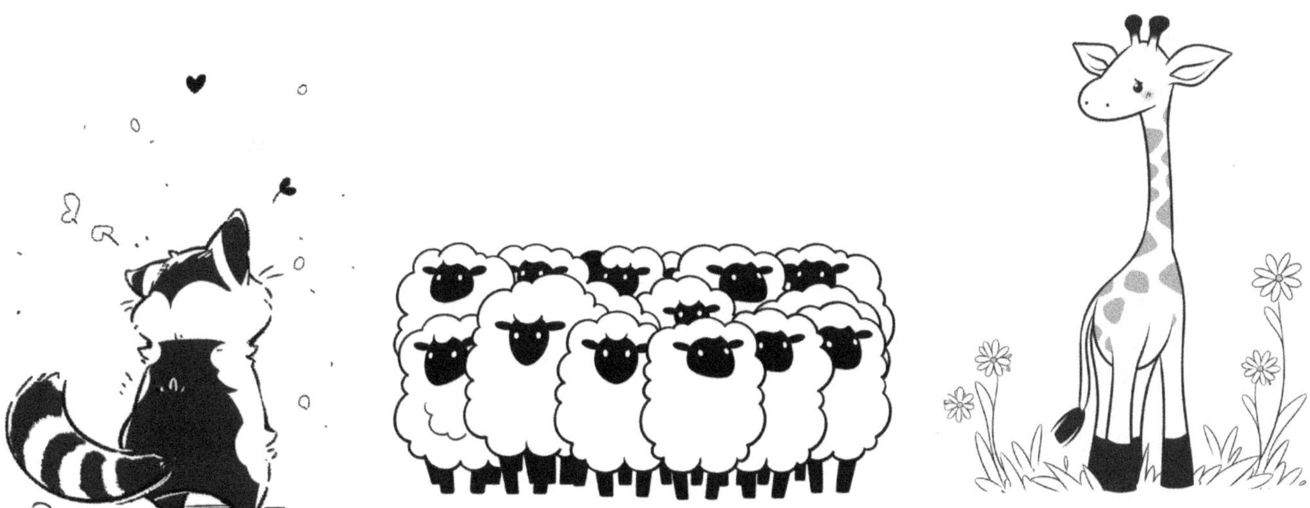

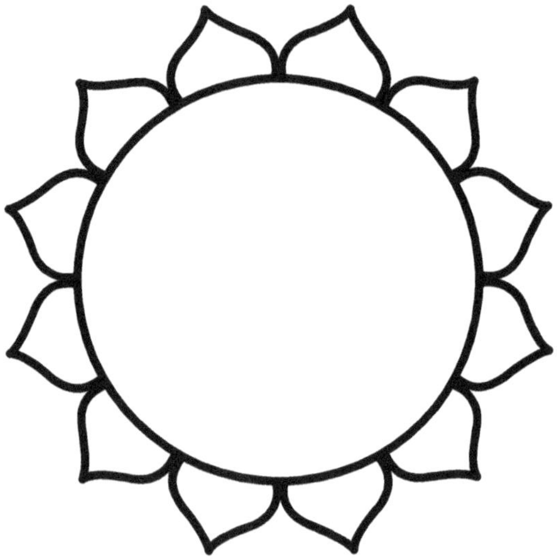

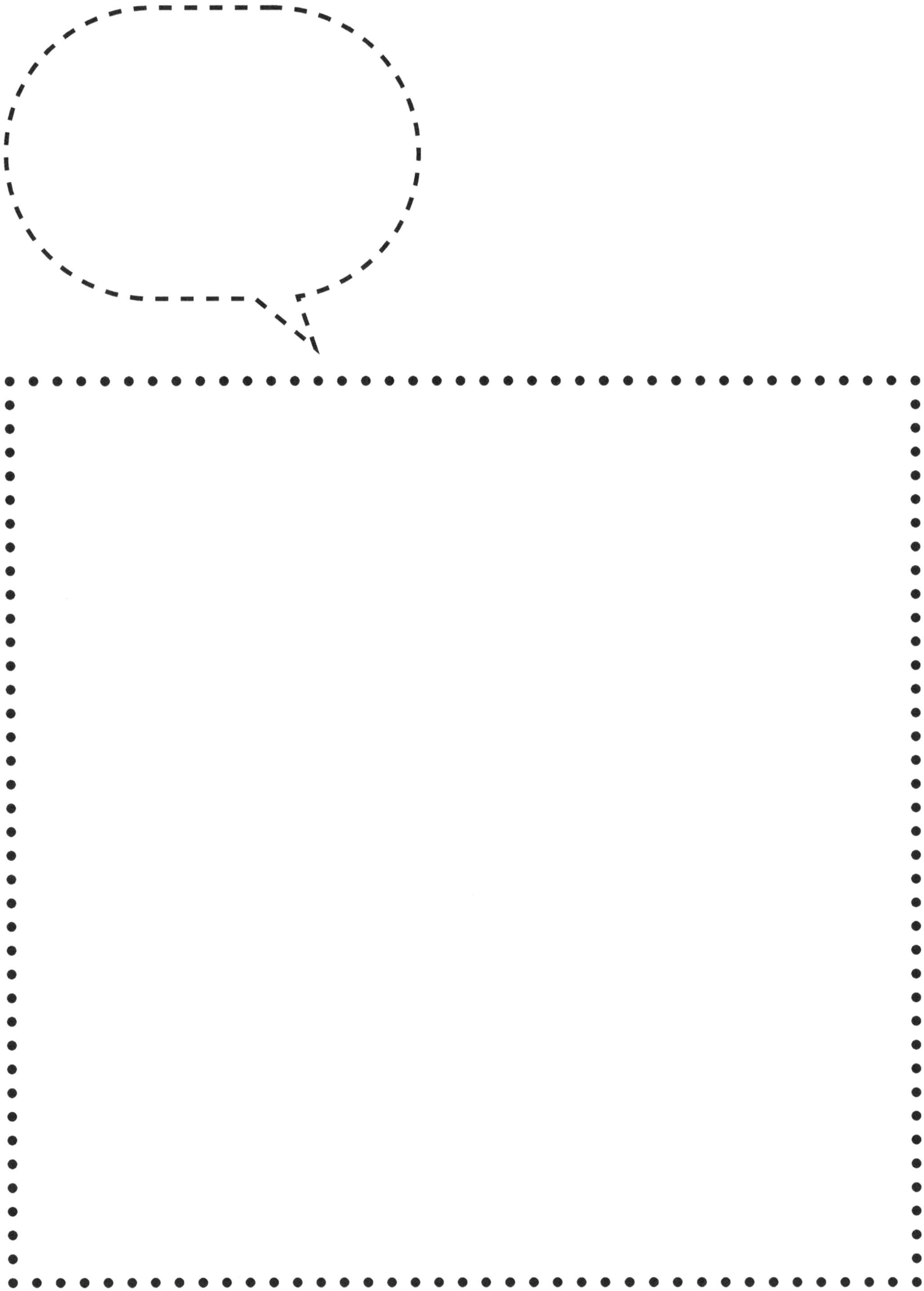

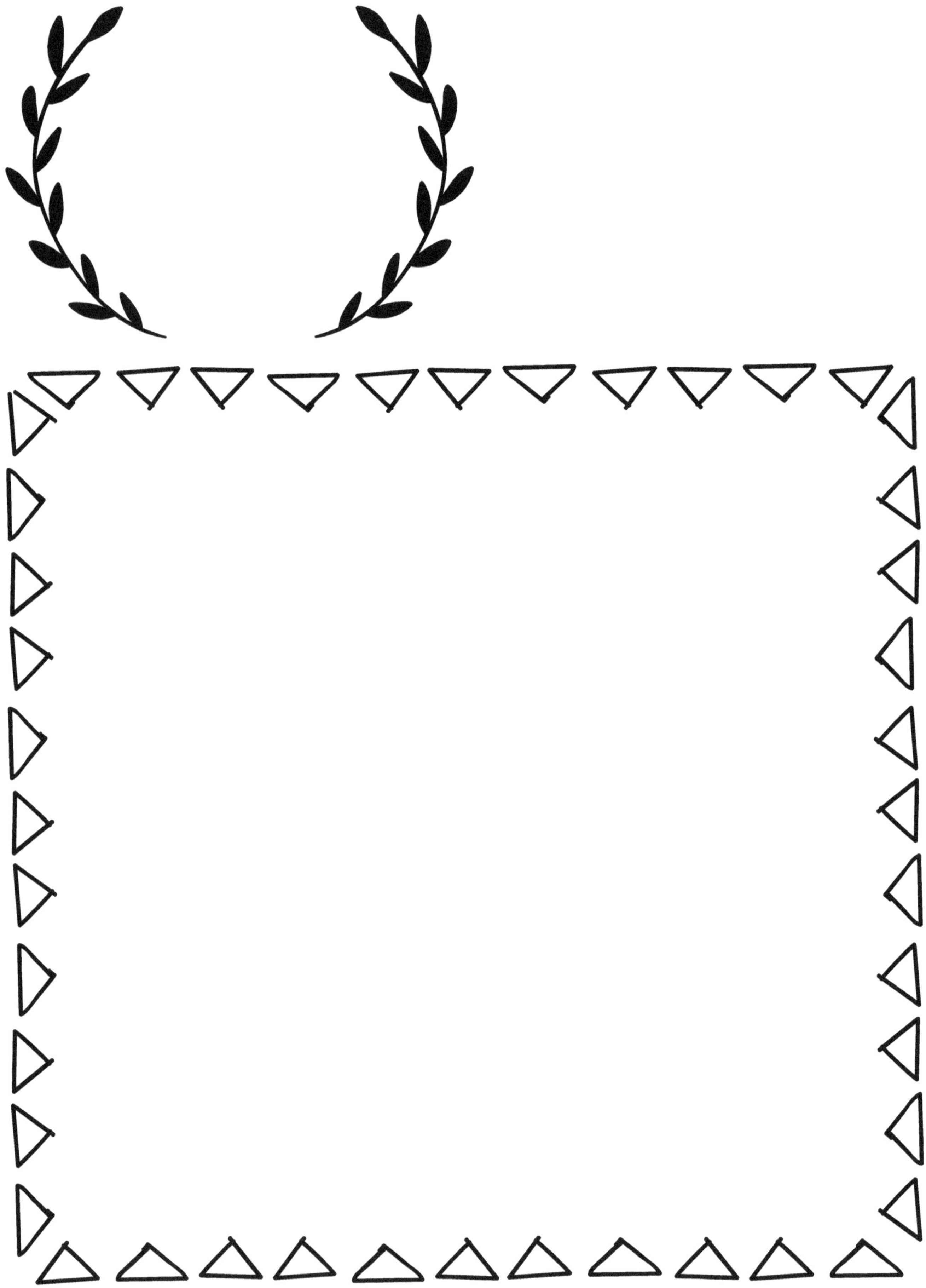

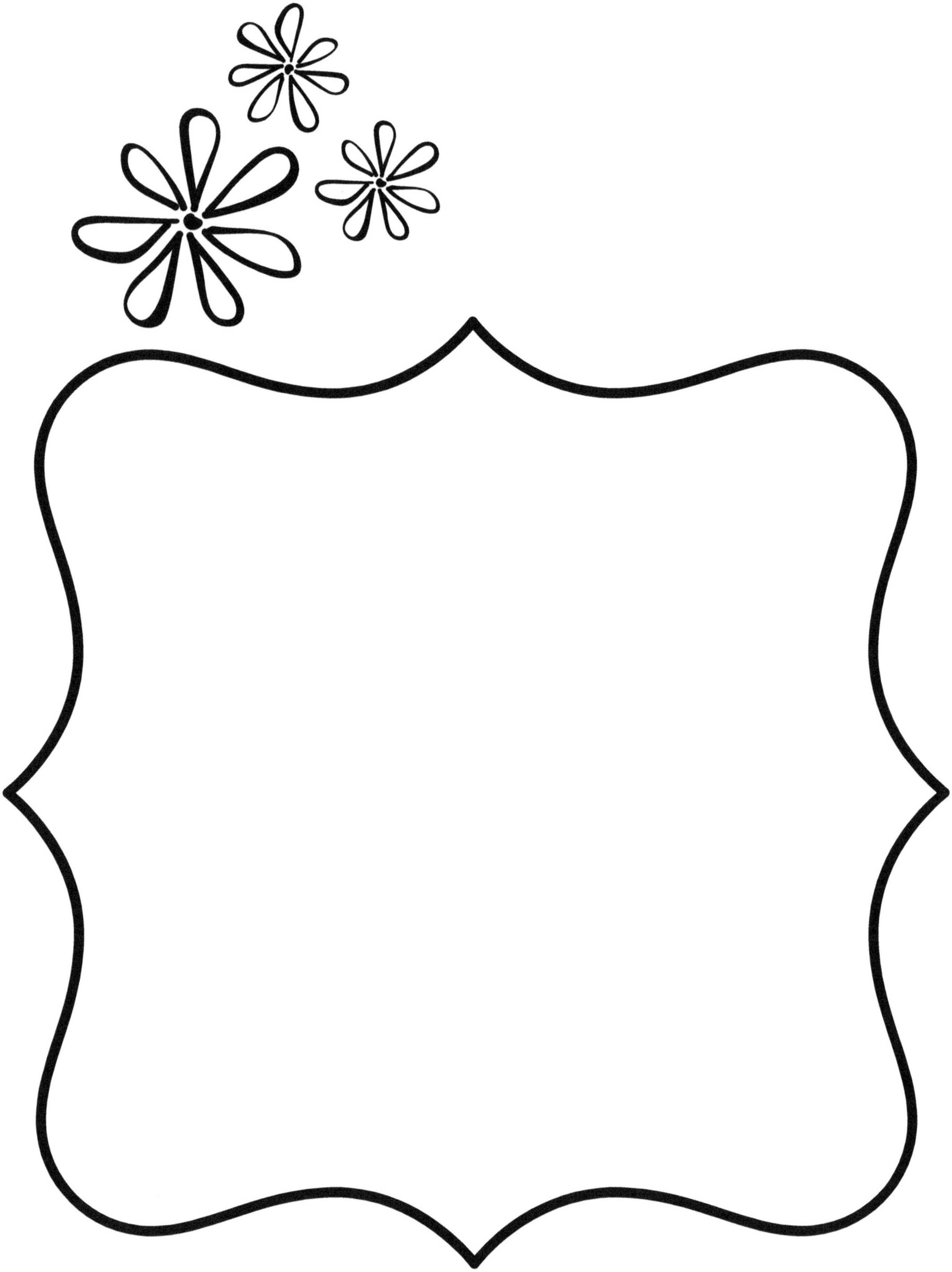

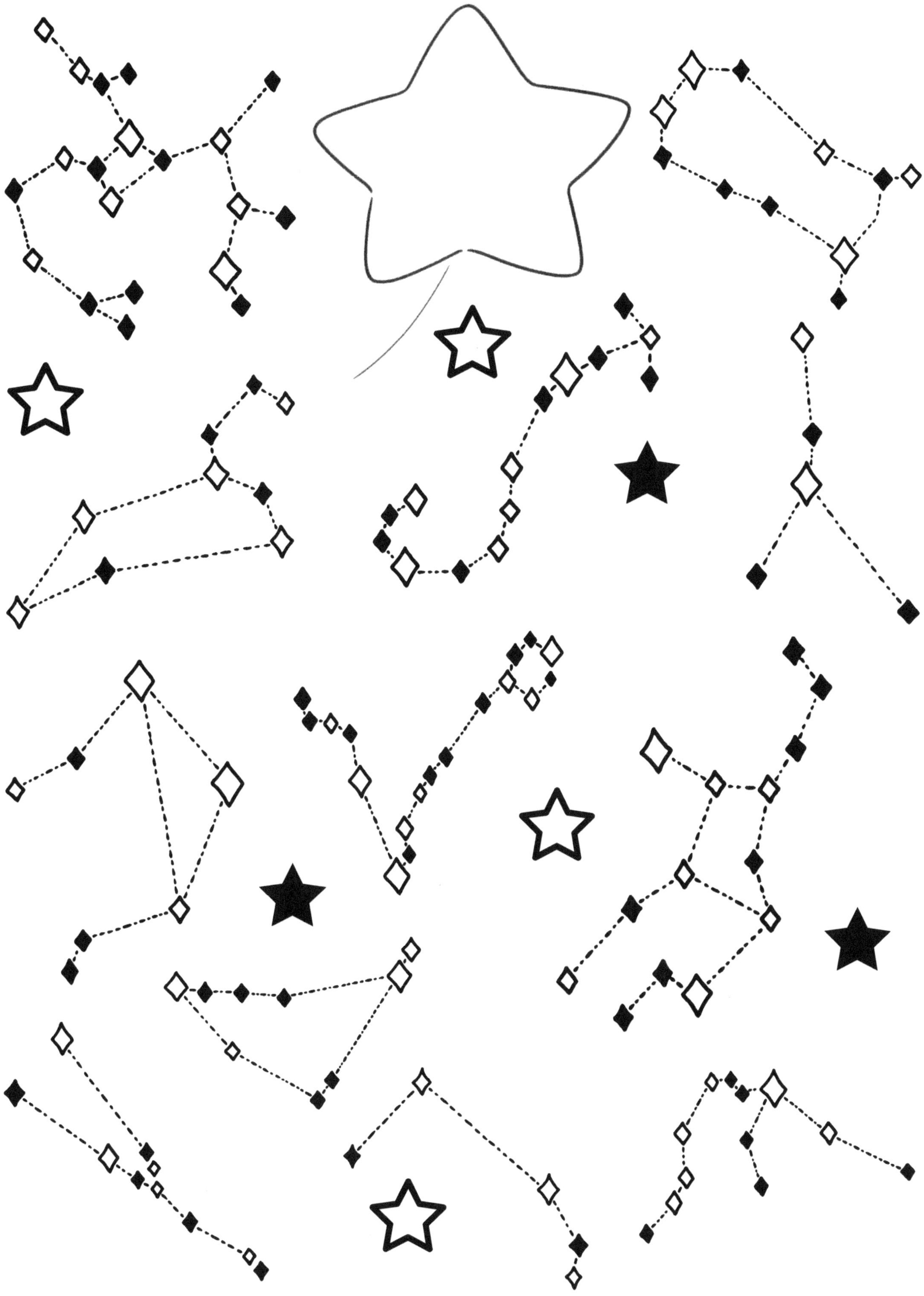

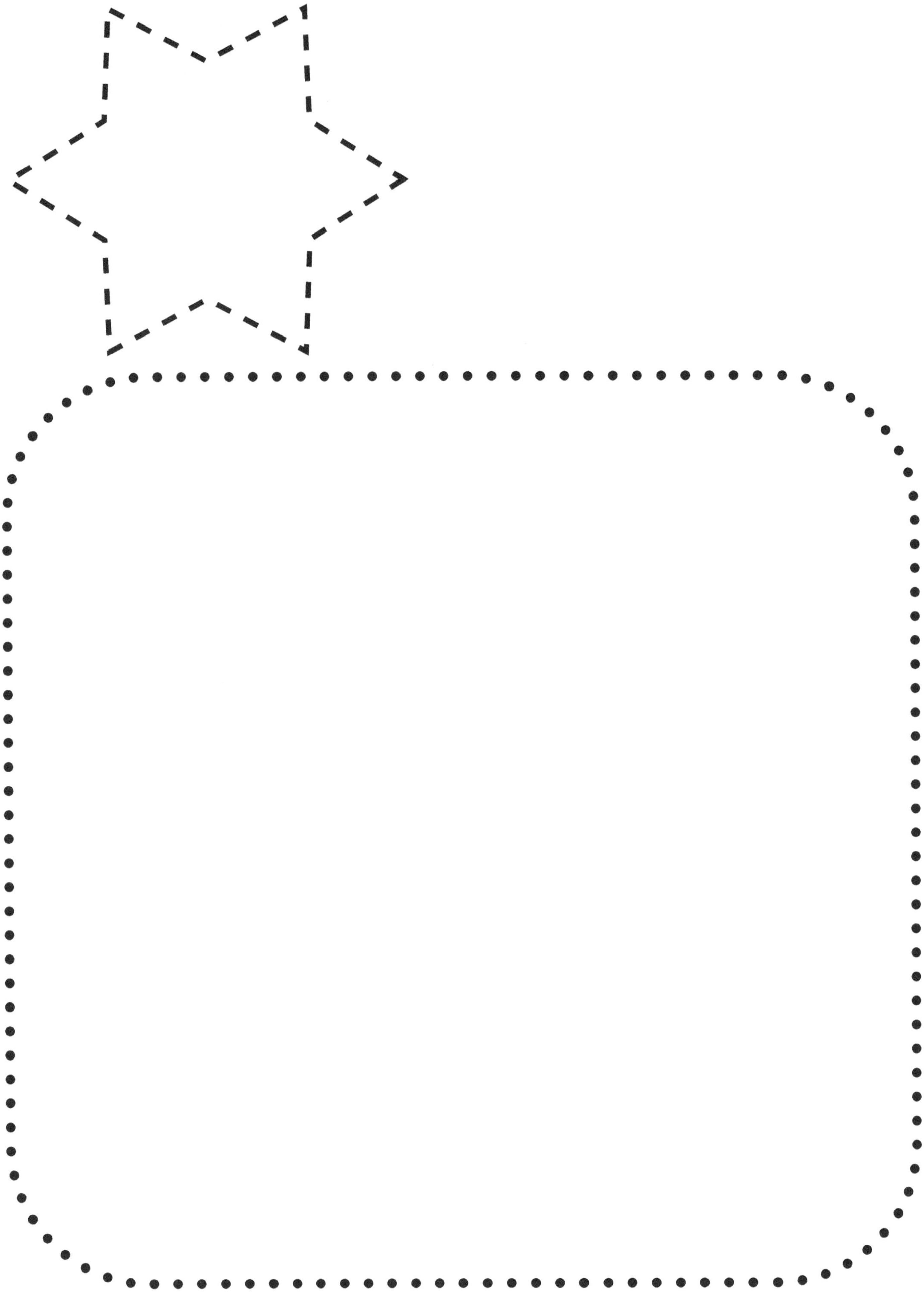

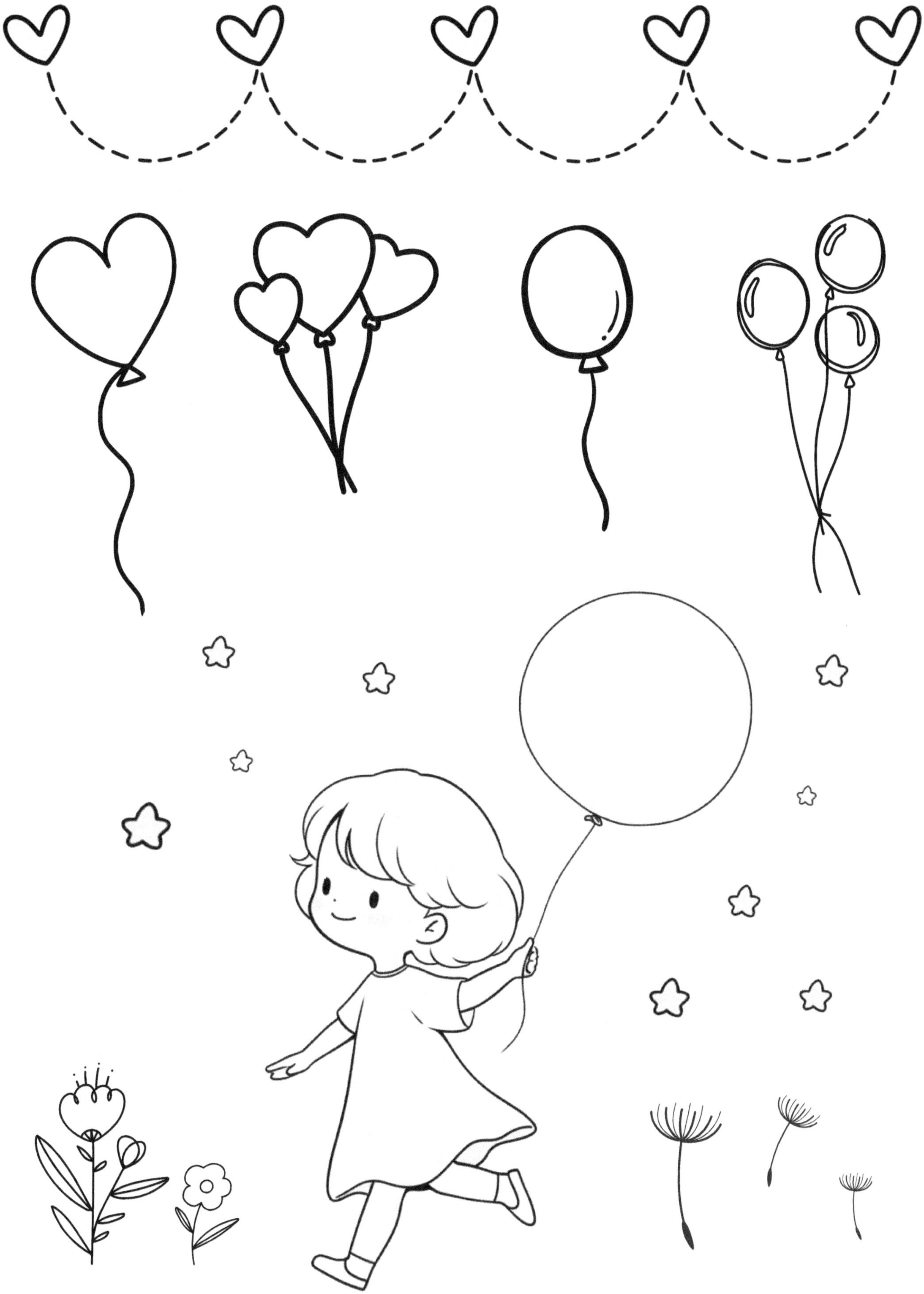

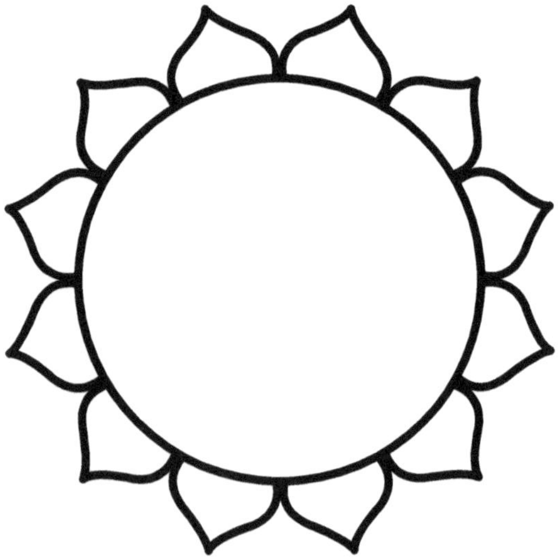

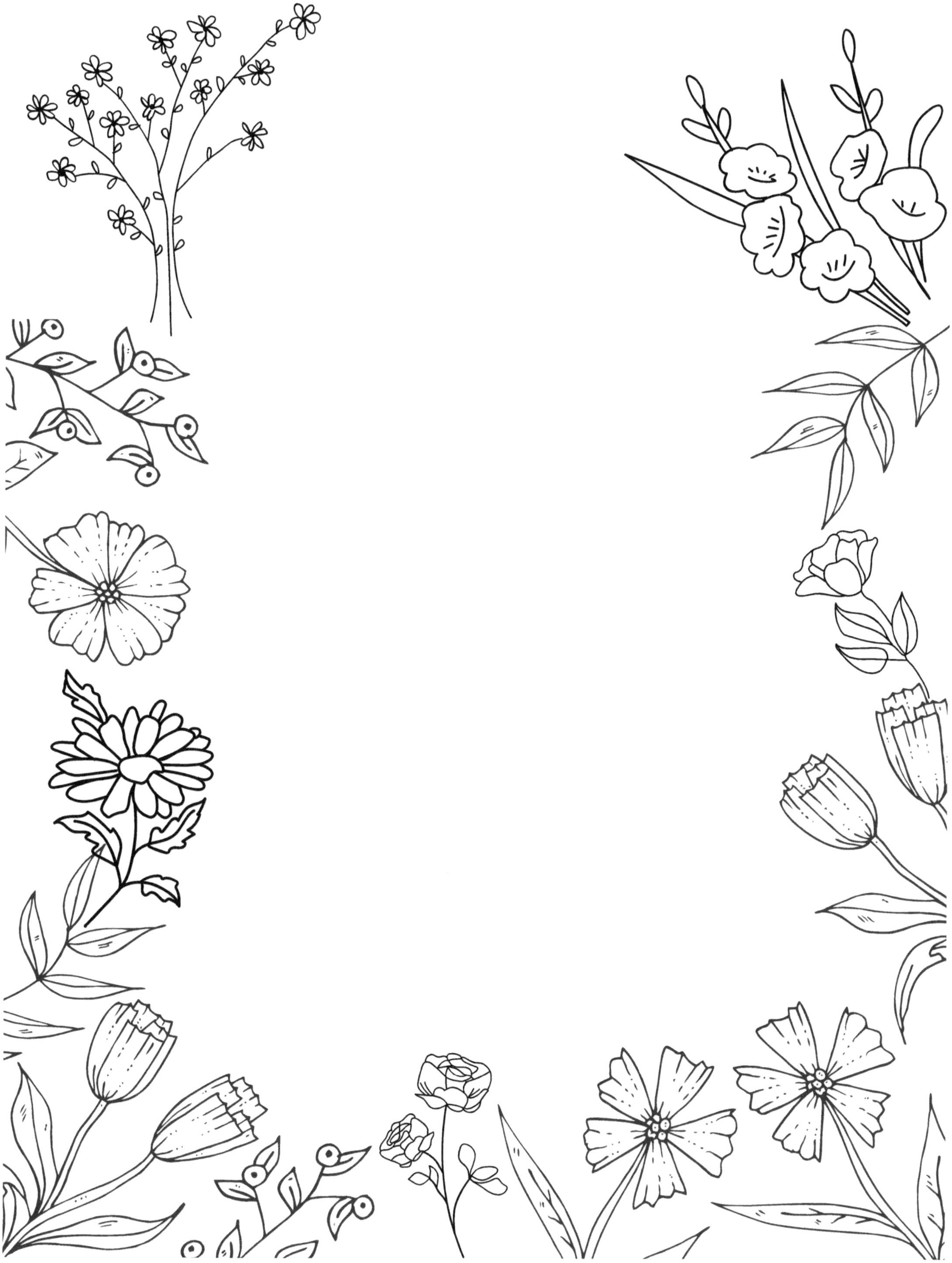

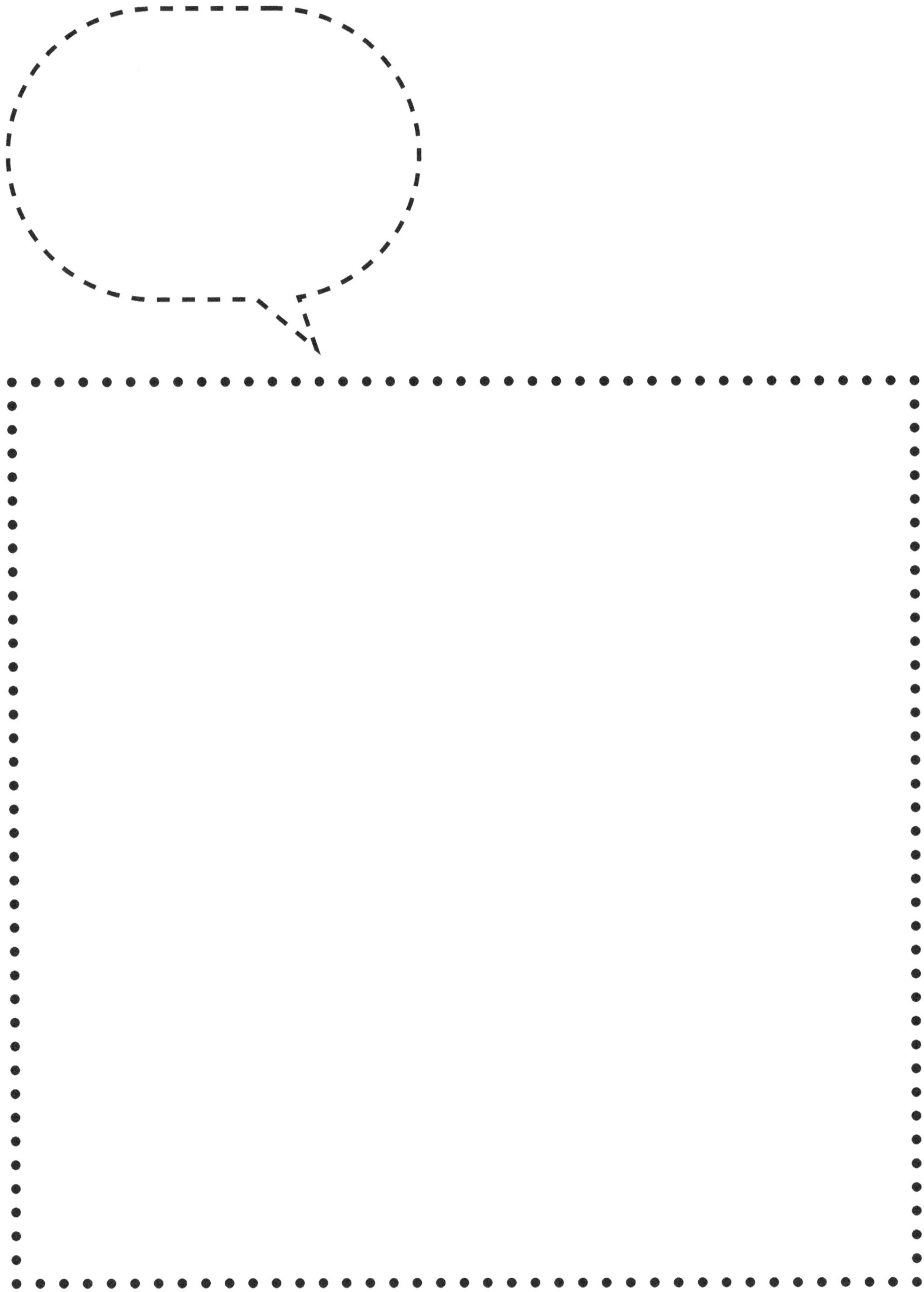

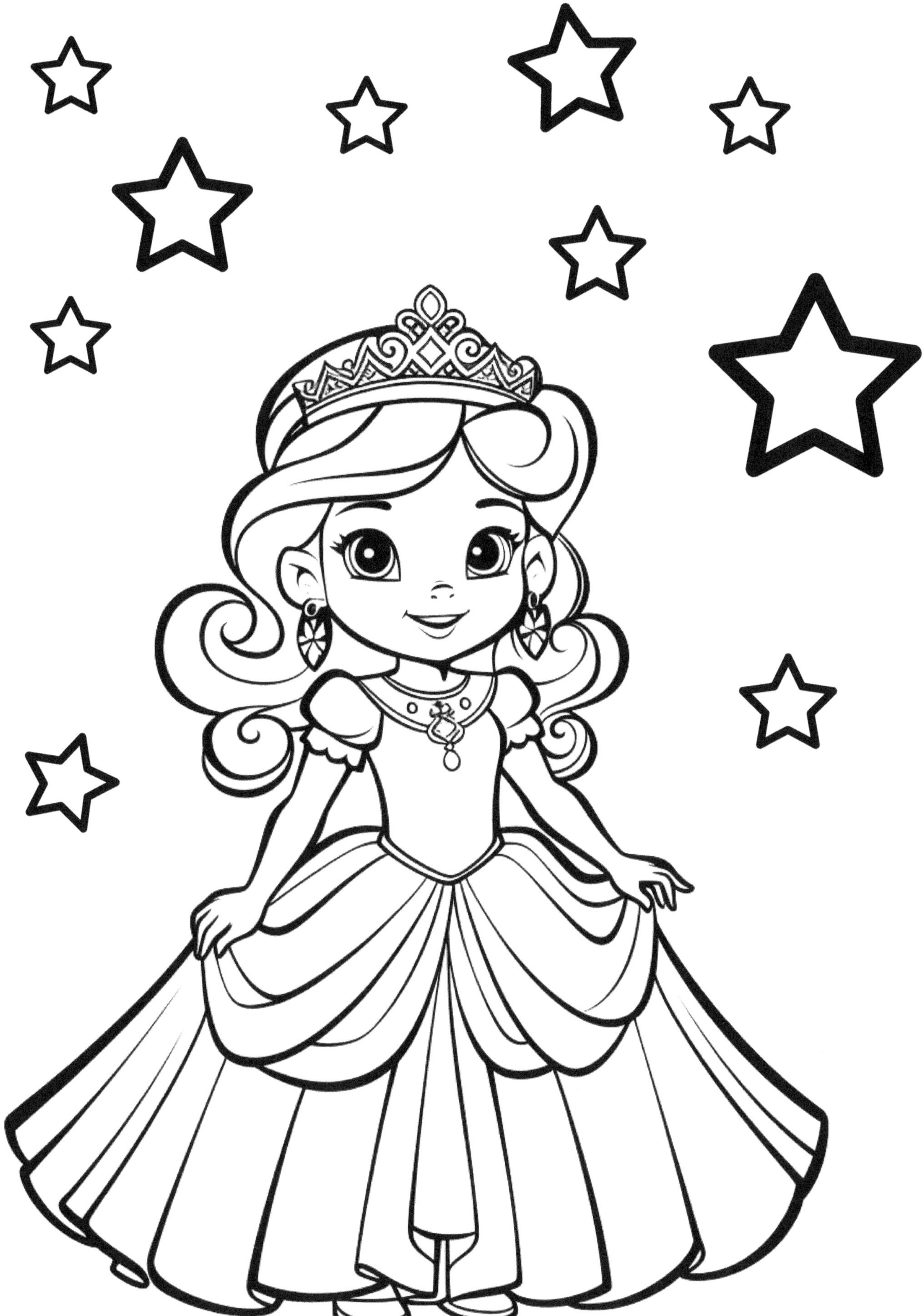

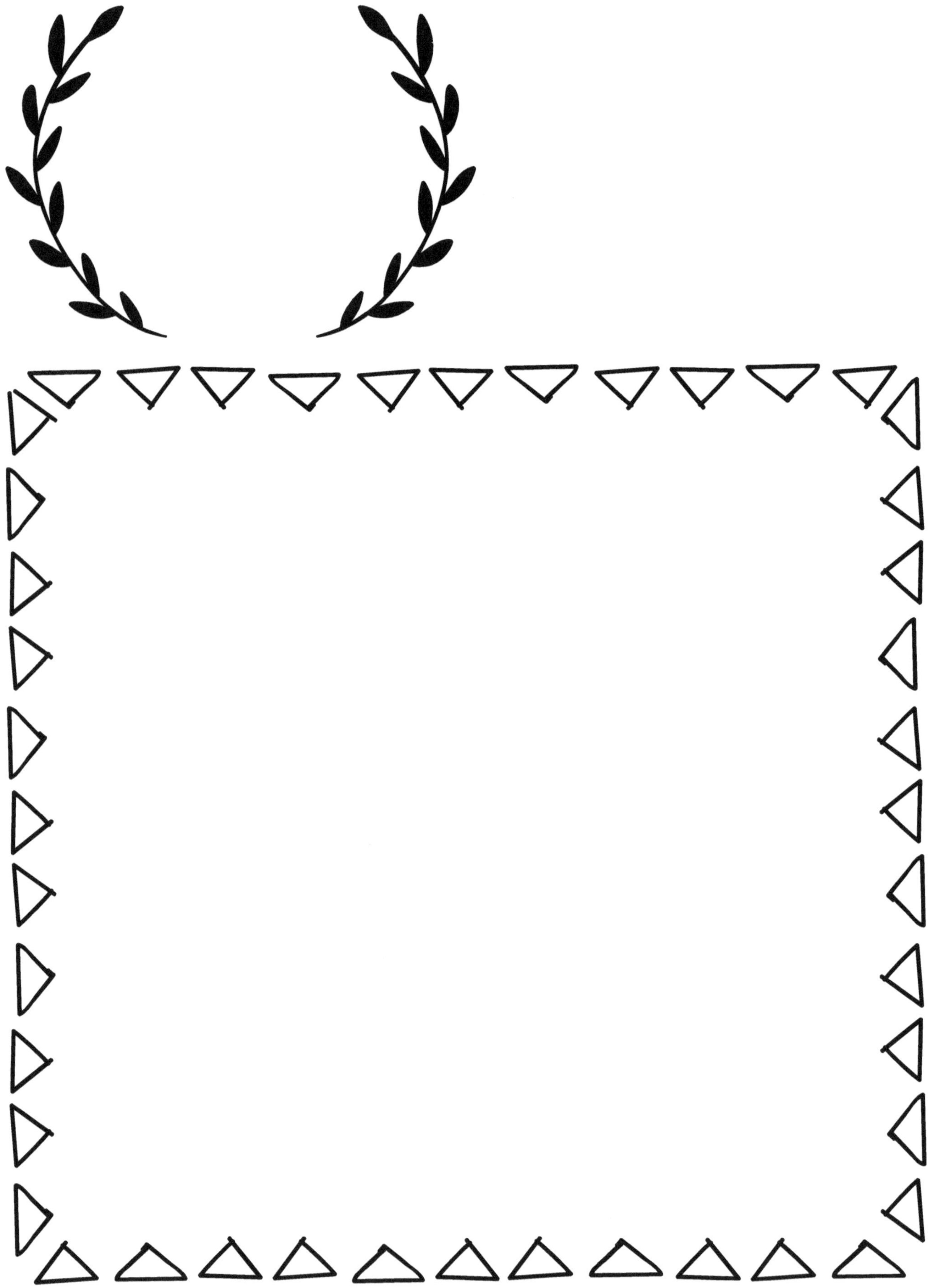